Dad

from Susa

This edition published in 2014 by

Pen & Sword Military
An imprint of
Pen & Sword Books Ltd
47 Church Street
Barnsley
South Yorkshire
S70 2AS

This book was first published as 'The Fife and Forfar Yeomanry'
by John Murray, Ablemarle Street, London, 1921.

Copyright © Coda Books Ltd.
Published under licence by Pen & Sword Books Ltd.

ISBN: 9781473823327

A CIP catalogue record for this book is available from the British Library

Printed and bound in England
By CPI Group (UK) Ltd, Croydon, CR0 4YY

Pen & Sword Books Ltd incorporates the imprints of Pen & Sword Aviation, Pen & Sword Family
History, Pen & Sword Maritime, Pen & Sword Military, Pen & Sword Discovery, Pen & Sword
Politics, Pen & Sword Atlas, Pen & Sword Archaeology, Wharncliffe Local History, Wharncliffe
True Crime, Wharncliffe Transport, Pen & Sword Select, Pen & Sword Military Classics, Leo
Cooper, The Praetorian Press, Claymore Press, Remember When, Seaforth Publishing and
Frontline Publishing

For a complete list of Pen & Sword titles please contact
PEN & SWORD BOOKS LIMITED
47 Church Street, Barnsley, South Yorkshire, S70 2AS, England
E-mail: enquiries@pen-and-sword.co.uk
Website: www.pen-and-sword.co.uk

CONTENTS

FOREWORD

MAJOR OGILVIE has done me the honour of asking me to write a short preface to a work which to me is of peculiar interest.

To write a preface - and especially a short one - is a somewhat difficult task, but my intense pride in, and admiration for, the part played by the Battalion with which the gallant author was so long and honourably associated must be my excuse for undertaking to do my best.

From his stout record as a soldier the author's qualifications to write this history are undoubted. His readers will be able to follow from start to glorious finish of the Great War the fortunes of that gallant little band of Fife and Forfar Yeomen who ultimately became the 14th (Fife and Forfar Yeomanry) Battalion The Royal Highlanders.

There was little of moment in the operations of the Egyptian Expeditionary Force in which this unit did not take part. In divers theatres of war they answered the call of Empire - from Gallipoli to Jerusalem, from Jerusalem to France - ever upholding the honour of their King and Country and the best traditions of the British Army.

No matter what by-path of the Great War they trod they bore themselveswith the undaunted spirit of their forefathers.

The experiences of the Battalion were so full of interest as to seem well worth placing on record - quite apart from the military importance of the operations in which they were concerned.

The ordinary reader must consider the conditions under which the work of this unit was carried out - often under a burning sun and again in bitter cold, mud and torrential rain - conditions which might well appal the stoutest heart, but here I note that the gallant author, as I expected, makes light of the many hardships and vicissitudes that he and his comrades were called upon to endure.

Again, when we consider how these heroes first entered the lists as cavalry, were then called upon to serve as dismounted cavalry, and finally as infantrymen, it surely speaks highly for that "will to win" that they had not long before the cessation of hostilities died of a broken heart!

Many a time during the two years that I had the honour to command the 74th (Yeomanry) Division both in Palestine and France, I noted - not without a feeling of intense pride - the cheery "never-say-die" spirit which pervaded all ranks of this splendid Battalion.

No matter what task was set them - no matter what the difficulties and privations to be encountered - all was overcome by that unfaltering determination and unswerving loyalty which carried them triumphant wherever the fates called them.

In conclusion of these few poor remarks of mine, let me congratulate the author on his story. If others read it with the same interest and enjoyment with which it has filled me, I can only think that the author's labours have not been in vain.

Further, may these remarks go forth, not only as a token to my old friends of the 14th Battalion The Royal Highlanders, of the admiration, affection, and gratitude of their old Commander, but to the whole of Scotland as a tribute to the memory of those good and gallant comrades of the "Broken Spur" whom we left behind in foreign lands.

ERIC S. GIRDWOOD,
(late) Major-General,
Commanding 74th (Yeomanry) Division.

PORTSMOUTH,
20th August, 1921

INTRODUCTION

THIS SHORT HISTORY, written by request, was started shortly after the Regiment was disbanded. For the delay in publishing it, I must plead the great mass of inaccuracies which had to be corrected and verified, entailing a considerable amount of correspondence and consequent lapse of time. It has been compiled from Official Diaries and Forms, and from a Diary kept by Lieut.-Colonel J. Younger, D.S.O., without whose assistance it would never have been completed.

It will, however, recall to the reader's mind the strenuous and eventful days we spent together in a regiment of whose history we are all so justly proud, and whose career now as a Yeomanry Regiment is ended, and it will recall the gallant fellows with whom we served and many a gallant deed.

To the glorious memory of those whose graves lie in a foreign land, I humbly dedicate this book.

D. DOUGLAS OGILVIE.

April, 1920.

OFFICERS AT FAKENHAM, 1915.

(Left to right) - Lt. Smith, Lt. Rigg, Lt. Hutchison, Lt. Herdman.

Lt. Gray, Lt. Stewart, Lt. Marshall, Lt. Lindsay, Lt. Robertson, Capt. Osborne, Lt. Don, Lt. Cummins, Capt. Mitchell, Capt. Ogilvie.

Capt. Tuke, Major De Prée, Major Gilmour, Lt.-Col. Mitchell, Capt. Lindsay, Major Younger, Major Nairn.

Lt. Nairn, Lt. Andrew, Lt. Sir W. Campbell, Lt. Inglis.

- CHAPTER I -
AT HOME - 1914-1915

AUGUST 4ᵀᴴ, 1914, MARKS the end and also the beginning of two great epochs in the history of every Territorial Unit. It marked the close of our peace training and the beginning of thirteen months' strenuous war training for the thirty-seven months which we were to spend on active service abroad.

The Fiery Cross which blazed across the entire Continent caught most people unawares and unprepared - but not so our headquarters. Our mobilization papers had already been made out and were despatched immediately on the outbreak of war. Each one of us was bidden to report forthwith to his Squadron Headquarters, and while we kicked our heels there, officers were scouring the country for horses. Soon these came in of every sort and shape, and in a week's time the Regiment was concentrated at Blairgowrie.

The headquarters of the Regiment was at Kirkcaldy, the four Squadrons A, B, C, and D having their headquarters respectively at Cupar, Dunfermline, Dundee, and Forfar. The recruiting area comprised the counties of Fife, Forfar, Kinross, and Clackmannan, and there was also a troop in Stirlingshire within a few miles of Loch Lomond. The rest of the Highland Mounted Brigade, to which the Regiment belonged, was pure Highland, consisting of two regiments of Lovat's Scouts, the Inverness Battery, R.H.A., and a T. and S. Column and Field Ambulance hailing also from Inverness. On changing to War Establishment, D Squadron dropped out and was divided amongst A, B, and C, with the exception of Lieut.-Colonel King who went to Remounts, and Captain Jackson who became Staff Captain on the newly formed Brigade Staff.

The Regiment was fortunate in having about a week at Squadron Mobilization Centres before uniting at Blairgowrie, and a pretty hectic week it was for most of us. The most rapid bit of work must have been that of D Squadron, whose men were distributed amongst the other squadrons, fully equipped, in about three days. This squadron was also called upon to provide the various details, such as mounted police, who were required on mobilization to report to the Highland Territorial Infantry Division, the famous 51st.

During this first week squadrons had to arrange for their own billeting, forage, and rations; take over, shoe, brand, and number the horses as they were sent up in twos and threes by the buyers; mark all articles of equipment with the man's regimental number; fit saddlery; see that all ranks had brought with them and were in possession of the prescribed underclothing, boots, and necessaries; take on charge all articles on the Mobilization Store Table as they arrived in odd lots from Stirling; and, beyond the above duties, which were all according to regulation, to make unofficial arrangements to beg, borrow, or steal clothing of sorts to cover those who had enlisted, or re-enlisted, to complete to War Establishment, and to provide for deficiencies in the saddlery and clothing already on charge.

The result of all the hard work was that it was practically a complete unit which came together at Blairgowrie about the 12th of August. Our Mobilization Orders had been thoroughly thought out and the general outline made known to all ranks, so that no time was lost in getting a move on. At Blairgowrie we were billeted in a school, and would have been very comfortable if we had been older campaigners, in spite of the fact that our horses were about half a mile away, up a steep hill, in a field which looked as if it had been especially selected so that we might trample to pieces a heavy clover crop, and at the same time be as far as possible from any possible watering place for the horses. It

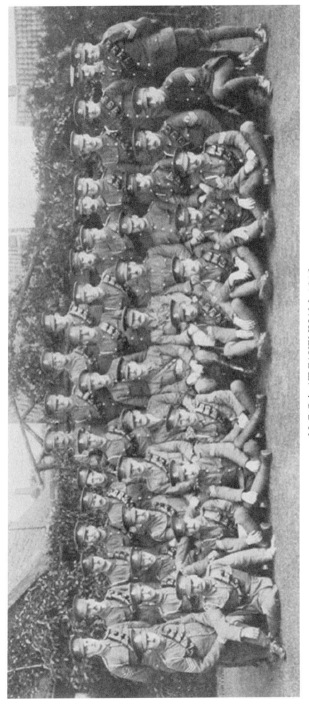

N.C.O.'s AT FAKENHAM, 1915.

Back Row (left to right). - *Sgts. Edmond, Petrie, Annand, M'Niven.*

Second Row - *Farr.-Sgt. Lindsay, Sgts. Inglis, Gourlay, Farr.-Sgt. Renton, Sgt. Abbie, Saddler-Sgt. Smith, Sergt. Kirk, F.Q.M.S. Allan, Sgts. Hood, Walker, Coltbart, Haig, Lumsden, Thorp, Dougall, Couper, Bradfield, Craig.*

Third Row - *Sgts. Thornton, Aitken, S.Q.M.S. Craig, S.S.M. Edie, S.S.M. Ogilvie, Capt. and Adjt. M.E. Lindsay, R.S.M. R.G. Rapkin, Capt. Jackson, S.S.M. M'Laren, S.S.M. Adams, S.Q.M.S. W. Birrell, Farr.-Sgt. W. Guthrie, Sgt. J. Wilson.*

Front Row - *Sgts. Scott, Stewart, Gair, Duff, Hair, Adams, Kidd, and Henderson.*

meant also about as stiff a hill as possible up which to cart all our forage from the station below. Here our adjutant, Captain M.E. Lindsay, who knew the whole business of regimental interior economy from A to Z, started to get things into proper form and to see that orderly officers, orderly sergeants, and orderly corporals performed as many of their proper duties as, with their inexperience, could be fitted into the twenty-four hours. By the end of three days order was beginning to spring out of chaos, and the adjutant never did a better bit of work - and that is saying a great deal - than he did in hunting all and sundry during those first few days.

A depot for recruiting was formed at Kirkcaldy and men quickly swelled our reinforcements there. After a few days at Blairgowrie, the Regiment entrained for the Brigade Concentration at Huntingdon; but as it was found there was insufficient space for a whole brigade, we were moved to St Ives, about six miles off, where there was a splendid common for drilling and good billets for the men. Very strenuous training occupied our two months there, and the expectation of going abroad at a moment's notice kept us up to concert pitch. An inspection by H.M. the King of the whole Brigade on the common at Huntingdon, and another by Sir Ian Hamilton, helped to confirm our expectations, and when we suddenly got orders one Sunday at midnight that we were to move to an unknown destination few doubted that we were bound for Boulogne.

What a bustle we had that Monday. We had built a fine range of stables on the Market Square, which were completed all except the harness rooms on the Friday, and on the Saturday all the horses were moved in except those in the sick lines. We had just received a consignment of about 100 grass-fed remounts which had been handed over to squadrons to look after, but not definitely allotted. Consequently when we received orders to move we had horses in the Market Square, saddlery about a mile away up the

H.M. THE KING, WITH BRIGADIER-GENERAL LORD LOVAT AND MAJOR-GENERAL BRUCE HAMILTON.

THE REGIMENT IN COLUMN OF TROOPS AT ST. IVES.

Ramsey Road, and horses in the sick lines which belonged to no one in particular and had never been fitted with saddlery at all. In addition, every one had been collecting every conceivable sort of kit "indispensable for active service," presents from kind friends and purchases from plausible haberdashers, with the result that quite 50 per cent. of our gear had to be left behind or sent home. To add to our confusion a draft arrived from our second line to bring us up to War Establishment, and they had to be fitted out with horses, etc. However, we got off up to time and entrained at Huntingdon, wondering if it would be three days or a week (at most) before we were charging Uhlans.

But our destination was only the Lincolnshire coast - Grimsby. Fortunately thirty-six hours terminated our stay there, and we trekked off south, eventually halting at Hogsthorpe, a village about three miles from the coast. The two remaining regiments of the Brigade were one in Skegness and the other half-way between us and Skegness.

For the next few months we moved from one village to another in the neighbourhood of Skegness. "We dug miles of trenches along the coast - we erected barbed wire entanglements for the sea to play with - we patrolled bleak stretches of coast day and night, and in all sorts of weather - we watched patiently for spies and Zeppelins, and we were disappointed. Nothing happened; the Germans would not come."

Christmas was spent at Skegness, and in spite of alarms and excursions we had an excellent regimental dinner, very largely due to the generosity of our friends in Scotland. The ladies of the Regiment opened subscription lists for "Comforts" for the Regiment, and everyone who was asked not only gave but gave generously. Wherever we went our "Comforts" followed us, whatever we asked for we got and, except on Gallipoli, we were never without our own private stock of Grant's or Inglis' oatmeal. We owe a lot to the generosity of our friends in Scotland.

CROSSING THE BRIDGE, ST IVES.

LIEUT. R.G.O. HUTCHISON AND MACHINE GUN SECTION, 1915.

From Lincolnshire we moved again south to Norfolk. King's Lynn was found to be unsatisfactory as a billeting area, so we trekked on to Fakenham which proved to be our final resting place in England. By now our training had so far advanced that we were not kept at it quite so hard, and we had more time for sports. We had polo, cricket, and all kinds of games, and on 3rd June mounted sports which were most successful.

We spent the summer putting on the finishing touches, and did some very useful bits of training, including some fairly ambitious schemes of trench digging and planning, which proved invaluable later on, and which was a branch of knowledge in which many Yeomanries were conspicuously lacking. Also, by this time, a few courses of instruction had been started at the larger military centres, and we had several officers and men trained at these courses in musketry and other branches who were then able to pass their information on to the rest of us. We were given an army gymnastic instructor who brushed up our physical training - on which we had always been very keen - and also started to put us through a thorough course of bayonet fighting. There was also a busy time among our machine gunners, who trained spare teams up to nearly three times our establishment, which was invaluable, as it enabled us to take advantage of the chance which came to us of going abroad with six machine guns per regiment instead of three. As our usual role on Gallipoli was to take over with three squadrons, whose effective strength was never more than 100 each at the most, and generally considerably less, from four companies of infantry, each numbering anything from 150 to 180 strong, these extra machine guns were worth their weight in gold.

By this time a good many were thoroughly "fed up" with so long a spell of home service, fearing that the war would be over before we got out at all. And it was not till nearly the end of August that we got definite news that at last we were to receive the reward of all our hard training and see service overseas. We

GUARD MOUNTING, FAKENHAM.

ENTRAINING HORSES, FAKENHAM.

were inspected and addressed by General Sir H. Smith-Dorrien. Our horses, that had done us so well on many a strenuous field day, that knew cavalry drill better than some of us, that had taken part in our famous charge with fixed bayonets on the common at St Ives, were taken from us and sent, some to our second line and some to remount depots. In return for a horse we were each given a heavy cavalry sword, presumably to prevent us being confused with mere infantry.

On 5th September we said good-bye to our friends in Fakenham and started off on our journey for an unknown destination but - business.

- CHAPTER II -
ABROAD - 1915

THE LAST FEW DAYS at Fakenham were busy ones, chiefly owing to the floods of new equipment which were at last showered upon us. Two squadrons got a complete issue of new saddlery, harness, and vehicles, which meant, in the first place, handing over the old issues to representatives of the second line, and in the second place, assembling all the new saddlery (which was issued in small pieces) and packing it into sacks ready for the voyage. The rest of the saddlery was put on board without being unpacked. Then our complement of machine guns was increased from two to six per regiment, which meant taking from each squadron 1 officer and 20 men to form the new personnel, and replacing them in the squadrons with men from the second line. By this arrangement we lost also our adjutant, Captain M.E. Lindsay, who was made Brigade Machine Gun Officer. Lieutenant H.S. Sharp took Captain Lindsay's place as adjutant. All ranks were fitted with helmets (on which pugarees had to be fixed under the eye of the few old soldiers who had been abroad and knew how to do it), and also with a complete outfit of khaki drill clothing. This last caused no end of trouble and annoyance both to the tailors and the men. However, it was all finished somehow, and it was a very cheery party which embarked on the train at Fakenham station just after dusk. The entire population turned out to see us off and wish us luck, and gave us a very hearty send-off.

Next morning we found ourselves at Devonport, where we were to embark on H.M.T. *Andania* (Captain Melsom), a second-class Cunard Atlantic Liner, and set to at once to load our baggage in the holds. Speed seemed to be the main concern, the safety of the cargo being quite a secondary consideration. The Brigade arrived in some dozen or more trains, each carrying what corresponded to a squadron, its baggage, which consisted of all sorts of heavy cases and things more or less breakable such as personal baggage, and saddlery in sacks, and also motor bicycles and vehicles. Each train was unloaded as it arrived and its contents thrown holus-bolus into one of the holds, except for the wheeled vehicles. The result was that there were layers of saddles at the very bottom of the hold, and further layers at intervals up to the top sandwiched between ammunition and heavy cases of all kinds. Fortunately we were never asked to unpack the saddlery.

On Wednesday, 8th September, about 5 A.M., we left the harbour escorted by two destroyers who took us to abreast Cape Ushant and there left us.

The first day or two on board was regular pandemonium and most uncomfortable for the men. Four officers and 140 other ranks from the second line had joined us at Devonport and we were very overcrowded. Each man had a stuffy and inaccessible bunk and a place at a table in the steerage saloon for meals, which had to be served in three relays owing to the numbers on board. This meant either very perfect time keeping or very perfect chaos, and, needless to say, for the first few days it was the latter. The captain also had a habit of always having his alarm boat drills while some relay was feeding, which did not add to the harmony. After a few days, however, things went very much more smoothly, but at no time could it be called a comfortable voyage. For the officers it was very different. They were not too overcrowded and were fed like fighting cocks. The deck accommodation was, of course, ridiculously inadequate, and muster parades, boat drill, and physical drill in relays was all that could be managed. We also had lectures on flies, sanitation, and how to behave when we got to Constantinople.

We steered a very roundabout course to avoid submarines and came into the Straits of Gibraltar from the south-west keeping well south of the Rock. We hugged the north coast of Africa, and passed a Greek tramp who signalled to us to stop as a large enemy submarine was ten miles east of us. As such ships had been used before as decoys for German submarines, we gave her a wide berth and informed Gibraltar who were to send out a destroyer to have a look at her. We reached Malta on 14th September, but we were too late to get into Valetta Harbour, so we anchored in St Paul's Bay for the night and got into Valetta Harbour early next morning. For most of us it was our first glimpse of the Near East, and no one could deny the beauty of the scene - the harbour full of craft of all sorts down to the tiny native skiff, and crowned by the old Castle of St Angelo, the picturesque town, the palm trees, and the motley crowd of natives swimming and diving, and hawking fruit and cigarettes from their boats. Some of us got ashore to see the historical old town, full of memories of the Templars - St John's Cathedral, the Governor's Palace, the Armoury - but most had to stay on board to bargain and argue with the native vendors. We slipped out of the harbour at dusk, showing no lights, but to show we were not downhearted, Lovat's entire pipe band started to play. But not for long; as the captain threatened to put them all in irons, which brought the concert to an abrupt conclusion.

We reached Alexandria on the morning of the 18th, and the first stage of our trip was over - to everyone's regret. We had had a lovely voyage, a calm sea and perfect weather, and only the most persevering had managed to get seasick. Those of us who had still lingering hopes of seeing horses at Alexandria were speedily disillusioned, as we were ordered promptly to unload all our saddlery and transport vehicles. This was done with just as much organisation and care as the loading. The following morning we all went a route march for a couple of hours through the town. Perhaps the intention was to squash any desire we might have had to linger on in Alexandria. All the same some bits undoubtedly stank less than others.

Meanwhile stacks of infantry web equipment had come aboard, and fortunately for us about forty infantry officers who were able to show us how to put it together. That kept us busy for the next few days.

A cruiser met us in the Grecian Archipelago and conducted us safely into Mudros Harbour on 23rd September. It had got very much colder as we got farther north, and the day before we made Mudros it was absolutely arctic, which was lucky indeed as it made us all take on to the Peninsula much warmer clothes than we would otherwise have done. Mudros Harbour was a great sight - British and French battleships, hospital ships, transports, colliers, and all sorts of cargo ships down to the little native sailing boats, and the steam cutters which tore up and down all day looking very busy. The island itself looked very uninviting, stony, barren, and inhospitable, and a route march only confirmed our opinions - the race ashore in the ship's boats, however, compensated us - and nearly drowned us.

Our ration strength at Mudros was 32 officers and 617 other ranks, but of these 9 officers and 63 other ranks remained behind as first reinforcements when the Regiment went on the Peninsula. Each squadron went forward 4 officers and 136 other ranks. When we returned to Mudros three months later our effective strength was 8 officers and 125 other ranks.

On 26th September the Regiment filed down the gangways of the *Andania* on to the A*bassiyeh* and landed that night on Gallipoli. From the A*bassiyeh* we were transhipped into a "beetle" packed like sardines and loaded like a Christmas-tree. These lighters being flat-bottomed could run ashore on the sand and land troops dry-shod. The gangway was very steep and slippery and the men were so overloaded, each carrying a bundle of firewood as well as full equipment, and a pick and a shovel, that nearly everyone, like

William the Conqueror, bit the dust on landing. Otherwise, we had an unmolested landing and started off for our billets in some reserve trenches about a mile and a half away.

Here our difficulties began with daylight, as we were in full view of the Turkish positions and within easy range of their guns, with the result we were not allowed to move about outside the trenches during the day. Water had to be fetched by hand about a mile and then had to be boiled, and we had not, like those who had been on the Peninsula a few weeks, collected a stock of petrol and biscuit tins for storage. Later on we even got water-carts filled with water brought from Mudros or Egypt, but not for at least six weeks, and meantime everything had to be carried and stored in petrol tins, rum jars, and such few biscuit tins as were water-tight. The wells were so congested, and the water so scarce that water-bottles were not allowed at the wells, and all we could do was to keep them in the cookhouse, ready to be filled and issued as the water was boiled. Apart from the November blizzard our first week in the reserve trenches, until we got our water supply in working order, was the most uncomfortable of our stay. Rations were really wonderfully plentiful and good.

That night we were ordered forward to complete the digging of a new reserve area. Just as we were falling in to move off, a regular strafe started in the front line only just over a mile away, but luckily it stopped just before we were to move off. It was our first experience of being under fire, and for all we knew it might have been the sort of thing that happened every night, so we just carried on as if nothing unusual were happening. Familiarity may breed contempt in most cases, but bullets singing about four feet above one's head is one of the exceptions, and Heaven knows we had plenty of experience of "overs" on the Peninsula. They are undoubtedly a fine incentive to work however, and once on the ground the men dug like beavers - and they *could* dig - and by dawn at 4 A.M. we had a continuous though somewhat narrow trench. The soil, for the most part, was clay, and it was tough work digging, but once dug the trenches stood up well.

After a day or two we began to be sent up to the front line for instruction, 30 men per squadron at a time, the remainder digging trenches and going down singly to the beach for a bathe. That was the one thing for which Gallipoli was perfect. The beach was rather far away, perhaps two miles, but we were all glad of the exercise, and the bathing was glorious - the water beautifully warm and so refreshing.

As regards the lie of the land and our positions there - coming up from the beach at Suvla there were fully two miles of flat country before you reached the foothills. The northern part of this plain was a shallow lake dry in summer but with a few feet of brackish water in winter called Salt Lake, and the southern part a few feet higher stretched down to "Anzac," where spurs running down from Sari Bahr to the sea terminate it abruptly. Our front line, generally speaking, was just off the plain, a few hundred yards up the slopes of the foothills, with any reserves there were lying in trenches on the plain.

Imagining the whole Suvla plain and its surrounding hills to be a horse-shoe, you might say the Turks held round three parts of the shoe, leaving us with the two heels at Caracol Dagh on the north and Anzac on the south, and a line between these two points across the plain. This plain was practically bare, but Caracol Dagh was thickly covered with dwarf oak and scrub, and Anzac with a good undergrowth of rhododendron, veronica, and other similar bushes. At Sulajik (the centre of the horse-shoe), and immediately to the north of it, and also round the villages in the Turkish lines, were numbers of fine trees, but nowhere that we could see was there anything that could be called a wood. As regards the soil, the gullies at Anzac on the spurs of Sari Bahr were quite bewildering in their heaped up confusion, partly rocky, but mainly a sort of red clay and very steep. In the centre it was a yellower clay with patches of sand and bog, and on Caracol Dagh it was all rock and stones, so that digging was impossible, and all defences were built either with stones or sandbags. The view looking back to the sea from almost any part of our line was glorious. Hospital ships and men-of-war, and generally monitors and troop-ships in the Bay, and on the horizon the peaks of Imbros and Samothrace reflecting the glorious sunrises and sunsets of the Levant.

In these surroundings we spent about a week before getting a turn in the front line. We struck a reasonably quiet sector and fairly well dug, but there were several details in which the trenches varied from what we were accustomed to read about. The first and most noticeable difference from the point of view of the inhabitants was the entire absence of head cover. Even after we had been on the Peninsula nearly three months all we had collected were one or two poles, a sheet of corrugated iron (ear-marked as a roof for a signal station), and a few yards of wire-netting. There was not a house or a building of course in the country-side, and as our neighbours were as badly off as we were, there was no scope for the enterprising.

Our first turn only lasted four days, and we had hardly a casualty until an hour or two before we were to move back into support. The support trenches were very much less comfortable than the front line, and as there were lots of parties to go up at all hours of the day and night to dig and wire in front, it took a lot of scheming to get everyone satisfactorily fixed with water and food. We also had to send out officers' patrols to fix the Turkish line, as we were intending to have a dash at capturing his barrier across the Azmac Dere - a dry watercourse which ran right through both the Turkish and our lines - and so straighten out our line. Patrolling was very difficult - there were no landmarks to guide one, the going was exceedingly prickly, and at that time the place was full of Turkish snipers, who came out at dusk and lay out till morning in the broken and shell-pitted country. We soon got the better of

GEBEL-EL-GHENNEIM, KHARGEH OASIS.

THE HIGHLAND BARRICADE, ASMAK DERE, SUVLA.

these sportsmen though - our snipers out-sniped them, and our bombing officer, if he frightened them with his catapults and other engines of offence half as much as he frightened us, must also be given credit for a share in dispersing them.

A squadron (Major de Pree) and the bombing squad under Mr A.C. Smith, in conjunction with a squadron of 2nd Lovat Scouts, carried out the raid on the Dere on the night of the 17th/18th October. It was a complete success - all the Turks holding the barrier being killed by the bombing party, and about sixty or seventy yards of new trench being dug the same night. This little exploit was the subject of congratulations from both the Divisional and Corps Commanders, Major-General W. Peyton and Major-General Sir Julian Byng. Mr Smith got the M.C., and Lance-Sergeant J. Valentine and Private W. Roger the D.C.M. for that night's work.

The Brigade was then due for relief, but we wanted to finish the job of straightening the line before we went, so we stayed on to the end of the month, by which time the work was practically complete. During this time we had the joy of receiving some letters and parcels, and even a very limited supply of canteen stores. People at home hardly realised as yet where we were, the conditions under which we were living, and the time it took for parcels to arrive. One officer received three parcels - the first containing his keys which he had left on his dressing-table at home, the second, some sort of collapsible boot-tree, and the third, about a three years' supply of Euxesis shaving cream. Many a good cake too had to be hurriedly removed and buried deep in the refuse pit. All the same, parcels were a great joy to receive, and provided many an excellent tit-bit for supper. Many, unfortunately, went missing - especially if they had the labels of Fortnum & Mason, John Dewar, or Johnnie Walker. We sometimes wondered if they were timid and preferred the comforts of the beach to the hazards of the trenches.

The canteen arrangements could hardly be called a success either. Occasionally a few supplies trickled through to us, and once

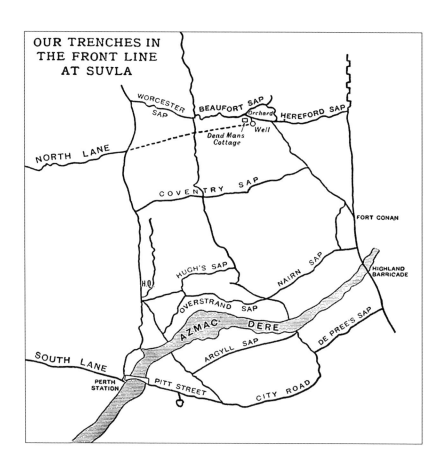

OUR TRENCHES IN THE FRONT LINE AT SUVLA

an expedition to Imbros was arranged to purchase stores at the local markets. Eggs, fruit, biscuits, oatmeal, chocolate, etc., were ordered by the hundredweight, and an officer sent to make the purchases. He returned to tell us the expedition had fallen short of complete success. His share of the plunder for the Regiment had been one packet of chocolate which he had eaten.

We had now completed our turn in the line, and were relieved by the 158th Brigade, and went back to our old place in reserve which we found very filthy. How we wished there were Dr Tukes in every regiment and battalion. He had so inculcated everyone of us - officers and men alike - with the vital necessity of cleanliness and the deplorable habits and peregrinations of the household fly, that we sometimes wondered if we were scavengers or soldiers. Though we lay no claims to perfection - or anything like it - few trenches were cleaner than ours were, and right to the very end of the war we never left a trench or billet without it being cleaner and more "lime and creosol"-ated than when we entered it.

The water arrangements had also been revolutionised, and we actually had cookers and water-carts in the lines, but the greatest joy of all was to go bathing again. The weather was not nearly so hot, and the flies which had tortured us in their myriads during the hot weather were now nothing like so numerous, which made it possible to enjoy what food we had.

Rumour as to our future movements meantime was rife. Lord Kitchener had come and gone, and all sorts of stories came from the beach. It was not till 26th November that we knew definitely that evacuation had been decided on, and that we had to make arrangements to get rid of all surplus kit and all our "lame ducks."

Meantime, we were busy improving our trenches and digging South Lane and Peyton Avenue communication trenches, and generally making ourselves more comfortable.

On 26th November we got orders to pack all surplus stores which were dumped, along with officers' valises, ready to be taken off that night by the Sikh muleteers. We parted with great reluctance from our tarpaulins and cart covers which provided the only shelters we had, but that night even they would have been of little use. At five o'clock the downpour started, accompanied by thunder and lightning, such as you only can see in the tropics. Thunder-clap merged into thunder-clap, each one noisier than the last - sheet lightning lit up the sky, north, south, and east at the same time - and the rain came down in torrents. It was a wonderful and awful sight. Trenches and dug-outs were quite uninhabitable and a foot deep in water. Fortunately by this time it was dark, so we climbed out of the trenches and prepared to spend the night on the top, where the water was only lying in places. Then came down the water from the hills. The Azmac Dere came down in spate, washing away the Turkish and the Highland barricades, carrying horses, mules, and men, dead and alive, down with it. Peyton Avenue and South Lane were culs-de-sac and soon filled, and the overflow flooded our trenches. The 2nd Lovat Scouts were completely washed out, and had to retire and dig in down near the beach. By this time the rain had stopped, and by next morning we saw the water subsiding gradually. Fortunately it was a misty morning, and we could wander about on top, though we did have one or two shrapnel bursts over us. We then discovered that our valises and stores were still floating in the water-cart emplacement - the Sikhs having turned tail when the storm broke. It was six weeks later when we opened our valises.

We had hoped the relief would have been cancelled, but not so, and at 5 P.M. we started off for the front line. The Turks evidently anticipated something of the sort, and their rifle fire soon forced us to take to the communication trenches. North Lane was not too bad. There was 18 inches of water, but the bottom was gravelly and the going not too bad. Where this trench struck the old support line we found guides awaiting us who took us past Willow Tree Well through the most awful trenches-too narrow for a heavily ladened man, greasy and slippery, and full of holes which took us up to the waist in water. Some idea of the going may be gathered from the fact that the journey of less than two miles took upwards of five hours to accomplish. And then our troubles weren't over. The firebays we found crammed with the infantry we were relieving - a helpless, hopeless mob - and it wasn't till midnight that we had the place to ourselves.

A Squadron (Major de Pree) held from the Azmac Dere to Fort Conan, and B Squadron (Major J. Younger) from Fort Conan to the old road leading to Anafarta, C Squadron lying in support. We could only man every second or third bay lightly, and our left flank was in the air - the 159th Brigade on our left, being about 120 yards away. Lovats were in, and to the south of, the Dere.

Movement in the trenches to promote circulation was impossible - one was exhausted long before one felt any life in one's limbs, and to add to our troubles snow fell during the night, and it turned bitterly cold. Next day was even more bitterly cold with snow and rain, and a lot of men had to go down the line sick with trench feet and exhaustion, many of them suffering from jaundice and diarrhoea as well. The area was again very heavily shelled with shrapnel, and we suffered a few casualties. By night time everything was covered with snow, but what really put the lid on was a sudden blizzard about 2 A.M. with ever so many degrees of frost. Everything one had on was of course soaking wet and covered with mud, and this was now frozen stiff by the frost. Most of the rifles were out of action, and even the water in the machine guns froze. However, daylight put new heart in us, and we made good progress in improving the trenches, getting rifles once more in working order, and generally tidying up and making things as comfortable as possible under the circumstances. That night about six or eight Turks crawled up the sunken road on our extreme left flank and caused quite an excitement, but finding the trenches still manned retired hastily. Unfortunately the message that they had retired miscarried, and headquarters stood to impatiently for about an hour.

Gradually the weather improved and the sun came out, and we managed to drain off more and more of the water from the communication trenches. But the damage had already been done - the wet followed by the cold and intense frost brought on trench fever in an acute and terrible form. One poor fellow had died of exhaustion and 142 left the Regiment in two days, some few never to recover and others to be maimed for life.

In the week following the storm 7 officers, including Major Younger and Captain Tuke, R.A.M.C., and 221 other ranks were admitted to hospital through sickness. Owing to the washing away of the Highland barricade, three men, bringing water up the Azmac Dere, foolishly missed our trenches and wandered into the Turkish lines.

By this time our numbers were so reduced that C Squadron was brought up from the support line and divided between A Squadron (Major de Pree) and B Squadron (Captain D.D. Ogilvie). A troop of Lovats and a section of machine gunners were in support to us. Later we were all amalgamated into one squadron under Major de Pree, 8 officers and 103 other ranks, the entire strength of the Regiment, including headquarters, being only 13 officers and 190 other ranks.

From the beginning of December we began gradually to send off parties of men to Mudros with surplus kit and stores. On 9th December we were relieved by the 2nd Scottish Horse and moved back into the support trenches, from which we sent a party back to the front line who reported very little firing from the Turks but that they seemed to be suffering from bad colds. Embarkation orders by Major-General W.R. Marshall were read to all ranks and we prepared to go. Three officers and 27 other ranks took over part of 1st Lovats' line and formed our rear-guard, and at six o'clock on the evening of 19th December the Regiment paraded for the last time on Gallipoli and marched to C Beach, via Peyton Avenue and Anzac Road. The perfect weather of the last three or four days still held; a full moon slightly obscured by mist, a calm sea and no shelling made the evacuation a complete success. The remains of the Regiment embarked on the *Snaefels* and sailed for Imbros, where they were joined by Captain D.D. Ogilvie, who had been acting M.L.O. for the evacuation and left by the last lighter. A four-mile march to camp and a hot meal, and our troubles were over.

The complete success of the evacuation caused quite a stir at home. From Suvla alone 44,000 men, 90 guns of all calibre, including one anti-aircraft gun, 3000 mules, 400 horses, 30 donkeys, 1800 carts, and 4000 to 5000 cartloads of stores had to be embarked - and only by night too, as of course the beaches and bay were visible by day from the Turkish lines. To deceive the Turks, men were actually embarked by night and disembarked by daylight to represent reinforcements, and the Sikh muleteers drove furiously all day chiefly to make the dust fly. On the last night about 12,000 men were embarked from A and C beaches, and everything had been so well managed that there was never a hitch of any kind. Needless to say each party arrived at the point where the M.L.O. were to meet them well up to time and were conducted straight on to the "beetles."

We were, of course, exceedingly lucky in the weather and in the lack of initiative on the part of the Turks. The Higher Command counted on 50 per cent, casualties but actually, on the last night, only two men were wounded on the way down to the beach - 8 old guns, rendered useless, were left behind at Anzac, 250 cases of Sunlight soap, a few Indian carts minus their wheels, and one or two hospital tents were left as a present for "Johnnie," and that was about all. The A.S.C. set fire to everything they could not take away, and a fine bonfire it made. The morning we left the wind rose, the sea became choppy, the Turks attacked in great style, bombarding the beaches very heavily, smashing the piers and nearly wiping Lala Baba off the map.

On 23rd December we left our camp and tried to board the *Prince Abbas*, but the storm was too strong and we had to land again. However, we got off next day, reached Mudros Harbour, and changed on to the *Scotian* on Christmas Day. None of us will forget the kindness with which we were received on the *Scotian*, and the arrival of a huge mail *and* plum puddings completed our joy. We left on Boxing Day and got to Alexandria on the 28th, where we at once disembarked and went to camp at Sidi Bishr.

Of the 32 officers and 617 other ranks who sailed from Alexandria on the 20th September, 8 officers and 107 other ranks returned on 28th December - each squadron on 20th September was 6 officers and 136 other ranks strong, the composite squadron on 28th December was 4 officers and 61 other ranks. On 9th December the strength of the Highland Mounted Brigade was 39 officers and 854 other ranks - the 2nd Mounted Division only 2200 all ranks.

In addition to the C.O., Lieut.-Colonel A. Mitchell, we had lost through sickness alone two squadron leaders (Majors J. Younger and R.S. Nairn), the Adjutant (Lieutenant H.S. Sharp) and his successor (Captain G.E.B. Osborne), the Quartermaster (Lieutenant W. Ricketts), and the M.O. (Captain Tuke, R.A.M.C.), the R.Q.M.S. and all the S.S.M., and S.Q.M.S., in all 18 officers and 339 other ranks. The Brigade was commanded by Lieut.-Colonel A. Stirling of Lovat's Scouts, Lord Lovat having left through sickness; the Regiment by Major J. Gilmour. Fortunately a good many of these, after a brief stay in hospital in Egypt or at Malta, were able to rejoin us later on.

- CHAPTER III -
EGYPT - 1916

FROM A MILITARY POINT of view 1916 can be summed up as far as we were concerned in two words - nothing doing. It was certainly for us the most peaceful and uneventful year. New Year saw us resting and refitting at Sidi Bishr - bathing in the Mediterranean and sightseeing in Alexandria. After a few days we moved to Mena Camp, under the shadow of the Pyramids, and at the end of the tram line to Cairo. Apart from the fact that we had two regiments of Lovat's Scouts on one side, and three regiments of Scottish Horse on the other, and every man was either playing the pipes or practising on the chanter from early morn to dewy eve, we had a peaceful time there for about five weeks, watching our numbers gradually increase as men returned from hospital, and wondering whether we were ever to be mounted again. That rumour soon, however, got its quietus, as we were told we were to link up with the South-Western Mounted Brigade (North Devon Hussars, Royal 1st Devon Yeomanry, and West Somerset Yeomanry under Brig.-General R. Hoare), and form a dismounted Yeomanry Brigade of six regiments.

On 12th February we removed up the Nile to Minia - a dusty, dirty, horrible place. Two expeditions of 2 officers and 43 other ranks and 3 officers and 40 other ranks set out from there - - one to guard bridges at Nazlet el Abid and the other to demonstrate along with Lovat's Scouts at Assiut. Minia is one of the wealthiest towns in Upper Egypt, and it was thought probable that the Senussi might attempt to raid Minia or Assiut, with a view to plundering the banks and giving a start to any disaffection among the fellahin.

On 5th March we moved again farther south to Sohag, and a squadron carried on to Kilo 145 on the Sherika line to take up an outpost line. Camel patrols were also sent out into the desert. We had a scheme or two in the desert and a fire in the M.G. tent, at which the local fire brigade greatly distinguished itself by its masterly inactivity and futile energy. To the strains of "Kam lêyâl, Kam iyyâm" at the far end of a leaking hosepipe, the fire eventually burned itself out. We only had two fires the whole time we were in Egypt, which was very creditable considering the inflammable nature of our "houses," and on both occasions our enterprising quartermaster made full use of the distressing occurrence.

We had two very excellent days of sports at Sohag against the Australian Light Horse and in the Brigade, our most popular win perhaps being in the tug-of-war. Another sporting event took place here - a racing camel, ridden by its Bedouin owner, was backed to beat any one of our officers' horses over a six-mile course, of which the first half lay along the canal bank, the last half over the desert which was pretty heavy going. After the first mile and a half the camel was leading by some 600 yards. After three miles the camel was leading by about 200 yards and rolling heavily, whereas "Charlie" and his horse were cantering steadily and easily. The latter continued to gain and passed the camel about the four miles, and won comfortably at a fast trot. In forcing the pace along the canal bank the Bedouin undoubtedly burst his camel.

We received a most unpleasant welcome at Gara on the night of 13th April. A severe sandstorm got up at night, and in the morning we had hardly a tent standing. Gara didn't like us. When we returned there in November we were washed out by a cloud-burst - a thing which hadn't happened there since the Flood.

On the 16th of April we went to Sherika, and there we remained till 15th November. We became a small detached force - the Kharga

Oasis Detachment under Lieut.-Colonel Angus MacNeil, 2nd L.S. Yeomanry, consisting of the Highland Mounted Brigade, a squadron of Egyptian Lancers, and a company of the I.C.C. Later on three 15-pounders were sent us, a company of R.E., a battery of Sikh Mountain Gunners, R.F.C., at Meherique, and later at Sherika about 1000 baggage camels and 2000 E.L.C. We also had an A.S.C. Bakery Section and our own slaughter-house, and towards the end of our stay at Sherika another company of I.C.C. joined us.

Our oasis which looked so green on the map, we found to be a deep depression of about 1200 feet, cut out of the central limestone plateau. On the north and east the drop was almost precipitous, and it was really a wonderful engineering feat to get a railway down it at all - only accomplished by means of unusually steep gradients and sharp curves.

The floor of the oasis is, for the most part, just as bare and desolate as the plateau above, but here and there are patches of green round the Artesian wells, which were the only sources of water. Except for the surroundings of the village of Khargeh itself, where there are a number of splendid wells, a small shallow brackish lake, and considerable date and fruit groves, no watered patch in the northern half of the oasis is more than half a mile long and a few hundred yards wide. The usual patch round a well would include a few date-palms, perhaps an apricot tree, and an acre or two of Bersim, the clover of the country, and a kind of Lucerne.

The groves of Khargeh produce great quantities of excellent dates, and a considerable trade is done with the Nile Valley in rush matting, made chiefly in the southern portion of the oasis, at Boulak and Beris.

Points of interest were the half-buried and utterly filthy village of Khargeh, the Persian Temple near Railhead in a very fair state of preservation, and the Roman Fort near Meherique. This was still

CAPTAIN TUKE ON "JOSEPH."

IN THE VILLAGE OF KHARGEH.

remarkably intact - a large square with bastions at the four corners, and built of mammoth bricks - about 60 feet high, with walls 12 feet broad even at the top.

The only notable natural feature was Gebel-el-Ghenneiem, which was just a portion of the original limestone plateau left standing. Its slopes were full of various sorts of fossils - sea-urchins and the like - so that evidently the sea had been there at one time. From its flat top one had a wonderful panorama of the desert.

War, with a No-Man's-Land of eighty miles and a very doubtful enemy at the far end, is war at its very best - even though we did have only marmalade and nothing but marmalade. But no war is without its horrors - these came about once a month in the shape of inspecting generals, who ordered us to raze our defences and build fresh and proper ones - not a bad game in sand, where you do anyhow see some result for your labours.

Every other week a squadron would go off to either Kilo 145, at the top of the Scarp, Meherique, the only place the engines could water, or Kharga (Railhead), and latterly to Water Dump A, to take over the outpost there with the I.C.C., or a troop of Gyppy Cavalry. Life there was not quite so pleasant on account of the mosquitoes (which, thanks to Dr Tuke, we had exterminated at Sherika), and the sand hill which formed the key to the situation at Kharga had a nasty habit of moving on and leaving our wire entanglements buried up to the neck. We owe a great debt of gratitude to Dr Tuke and his sanitary squad for the comfort and health of the Regiment at Sherika. At all hours of the day the doctor and his faithful mule waged war on the mosquito and the Gyppy sanitary squad indiscriminately, and with complete success. Fly and fellah, mosquito and reis - all fled at his approach, or buried themselves in the sand.

After the departure of Lovat's Scouts for Alexandria, whence they emerged as 10th Camerons, and proceeded to Salonika, the West Somerset Yeomanry joined us, and on 1st August two detachments from the North Devon Hussars and the Royal 1ˢᵗ Devon Yeomanry were attached to us.

The half section of guns - old Nordenfeldts - had arrived without a crew, but a couple of officers and one or two N.C.O.'s and men who had once been Territorial gunners took the matter in hand with great alacrity. Mobility was their chief trouble. Camel harness was produced - they were taken out a couple of days before a field-firing practice, and the targets were adjusted till the guns could hit them every time, and really when the inspecting general arrived they gave a most creditable performance.

We also had a mounted troop, under Lieutenant W. Gray, mounted mainly on mules for the longer patrols, and a Light Car Patrol (Lieutenant A.S. Lindsay) consisting of 2 officers, 45 other ranks, and seven Ford cars, fitted with Lewis guns, and one armoured car, which went out with the camelry. Lieutenant M'Dougal's bombing school and the rifle range combined instruction with amusement.

The heat during the day was very trying-as much as 120° F. being recorded in the shade - but we only worked from reveille (5.30) to breakfast, and in the afternoon from 4.30 to 6. Polo and an occasional jackal hunt, cricket and football, and all kinds of foot sports kept us fit, but the most enjoyable time of all was in the swimming-baths. When we first went there, there was only a small swimming-bath built for the officials of the Western Oasis Corporation, which was reserved for officers and for sergeants twice a week. However, with the help of the Engineers, we built a beautiful swimming-bath, 26 yards long, which was formally opened by Lieut.-Colonel A. M'Neil, O.C. troops, at a swimming gymkhana on 6ᵗʰ August.

Although we had abundant water at Sherika and Kharga, it had to be bored for. There was a river about 400 to 600 feet below ground, and the water came up quite warm - about 85° F. The problem was how to provide water for the 100-mile advance across

SENTRY ON WATER DUMP "A."

CAMEL LINES AT KHARGEH.

the desert to Dakhla. For this purpose the R.E. started boring at Water Dump A, about twenty-five miles from Sherika, and were so far successful that, at the finish of the Dakhla expedition, they were obtaining sufficient water to work the bore. By that time also the light railway had advanced to within a few miles of Water Dump A.

The campaign was brought to an abrupt termination through the overzeal of O.C. Light Car Patrol, who patrolled right up to Senussi outpost at the entrance to the Dakhla Oasis. At the sight of Mr Lindsay and his car the Senussi general fled, and when the I.C.C., after a very fine march, got into Dakhla, all they got were 197 miserable, underfed, diseased prisoners. Four officers and 100 other ranks from C Squadron (Captain D.D. Ogilvie), and 2 officers and 30 other ranks from the M.G.C. (Mr D. Marshall) set off on 25th October to relieve the I.C.C. It was a trying march. Cars dumped fanatis with water for the midday meal, twelve miles on and more for the evening meal, and breakfast seven miles beyond that. The second day out was a scorcher, blazing hot and no wind, over rough stony going for the most part, and Hell's Gate wasn't reached till 7 p.m., after a very exhausting march. The total march was seventy-six miles to Tenida, and of the 136 only 7 failed to finish which, considering the circumstances, was very creditable. No sooner were we there than orders were received to return again. This time, however, we went in cars as far as Water Dump A, and there we commandeered a convoy of camels returning with empty fanatis, and we finished our trek mounted. Great credit is due to the Light Car Patrol and to the Ford cars which really were wonderful. Neither sand up to the axle, nor dropping down over rocks stopped them - they made a road for themselves as they went along, and always seemed to get there.

That finished our 1916 campaign against the Senussi - the I.C.C. were relieved by a London Yeomanry Company of the I.C.C, and later on some Gyppy Cavalry went out and garrisoned Dakhla Oasis.

On 13th November the Regiment started in relays by train for Gara. There we received orders to start infantry training, as we were to be converted into a battalion of infantry. Till then we had always done dismounted cavalry drill. We now started hammer and tongs at infantry drill, instructed by an officer and two N.C.O.'s from a neighbouring garrison battalion. We were all looking forward to becoming pukka infantry, as we had long realised that in our eccentric form as dismounted yeomanry we should only be given the odd jobs.

We had just got our camp tidy when the water-spout burst, and not only washed out our lines and those of the Ayrshire and Lanarkshire Yeomanries, but also demolished the fine earth church which the Anglican Padre had had built.

On 1st December we arrived at Moascar, a large camp on the Sweetwater Canal near Ismailia, and there our infantry training started in earnest. We ate our Christmas dinner there, and on Boxing Day had Brigade sports. There was very fair bathing in Lake Timsah, and we all enjoyed getting a sight of the Suez Canal, and being once more in comparative comfort and civilization.

OFFICERS

C.O.Lieut.-Colonel.. J. GILMOUR

2nd in Command... Major J. YOUNGER

A Squadron ..... Major C. G DE PREE & Capt. R.W. STEWART

B Squadron..Major G.E.B. OSBORNE

C Squadron .... Capt. D.D. OGILVIE

Adjutant.. Lieut. H.S. SHARP

Q.-M. ....Lieut. R.H. COLTHART

M.O. .... Capt. A. TUKE, R.A.M.C.(T.)

SENUSSI PRISONERS, DAKHLA.

THE SERGEANTS' REEL, MOASCAR.

- CHAPTER IV -
EGYPT & PALESTINE - 1917

NEW YEAR'S DAY SAW the Regiment at Moascar Camp, Ismailia, and it was there that the Fife and Forfar Yeomanry were interred "for the duration," giving birth at the same time to a sturdy son - the 14th (Fife and Forfar Yeomanry) Battalion, Royal Highlanders. We were all very sorry to see the demise of the Yeomanry and to close, though only temporarily, the records of a Regiment which had had an honourable career, and of which we were all so proud. At the same time we realised that, in our capacity as dismounted yeomanry, we were not pulling our weight either as yeomanry or infantry, and no other regiment certainly appealed to us as much as our own Territorial Infantry Regiment, and we were proud to link our record to the long and glorious record of the Black Watch.

We spent five weeks altogether at Moascar, working hard at the elementary forms of infantry drill and tactics, and on 8th January we marched to our new camp El Ferdan, some ten miles along the Canal. Here we continued our training, but of a more advanced kind, brigade schemes, tactical tours and route marches, "jerks," bathing, and football kept us busy and fit.

One day some of us went to see the Canal defences, dug the previous year, about four miles east of the Canal. The sand was so soft, no amount of ordinary sandbagging or revetting would make it stand up, and all the trenches were made by sinking complete wooden frames into a wide scooped out trench, and then shovelling the sand back on either side of the frame. The original digging had to be about 20 feet wide to allow them to sink the frames sufficiently deep in the sand. It must have been a colossal work, and this was only a small portion of the scheme, which included laying on water to the more important defences, and laying out lines of light railways and roads from the Canal eastwards, at intervals of seven and eight miles, the railheads being linked by a lateral road.

On 4th March we left El Ferdan and marched to Kantara, the base of all operations up the Sinai Railway, and there entrained for El Arish to join the 74th (Yeomanry) Division. The journey of about ninety miles, over the very recently laid railway, was timed to take some eight or nine hours, and was uneventful and, though we travelled in open trucks, was not too unpleasantly hot. The frequent short gradients led to the most awful bumps and tearings at the couplings, but they stood the strain all right.

It was a very interesting journey to us, who knew only the Western Desert, to note the difference between it and Sinai. To our eyes Sinai did not appear to be a desert at all, as there were scrubby bushes of sorts growing in nearly every hollow, various kinds of camel grass, and even a few flowers - such as poppies and one or two species of lilies. After the waste of misshaped lumps of limestone and volcanic looking boulders, which were the only decoration of the Western Desert, this sort of landscape seemed positively verdant.

At El Arish we were camped some three miles from the station, and a very long three miles it seemed, as a large part of the way was over the softest of sand and most exhausting marching, especially with a heavy pack. Here we had our first sight of hostile aeroplanes, some of which came over nearly every day; it was a very pretty sight to see them in the brilliant blue at about 12,000 feet, with the white puffs of shrapnel bursting now on one side of them now on the other (but seldom very close). We were at once set to dig ourselves funkholes, which we were supposed to occupy on the alarm being given, but they never once bombed us, or seemed to take any notice of us. They made one or two bold individual

THE BATTALION MASCOT.

BATTALION COOKHOUSE, EL FERDAN.

attacks on the railway, between Kantara and El Arish, but for the most part they appeared to be out purely for reconnaissance.

At El Ferdan we had got our first infantry reinforcements - 11 new officers - and now we received a welcome addition in the shape of 1 officer and 373 other ranks, which necessitated the reorganisation of the battalion. We also had to acclimatise the new draft who felt the heat and heavy going very exhausting, and, to begin with, had to go easy.

Our camp was pleasantly situated on a sandy plain, within half a mile of the sea, and dotted with scattered fig-trees just beginning to show a few leaves. The climate was perfect, but the water arrangements were most difficult. We began to realise that it does not pay to be the last comer when there is a shortage of anything. We were paid off with the minimum number of fanatis (copper vessels for carrying water on camel pack), and, instead of getting allotted to us the wells nearest our camp, we had just to take whatever wells were left. These proved to be on the other side of El Arish village, in amongst the steepest sandhills, and it was a very tough tramp for the fatigue party, which had to accompany the water camels and do the pumping. Our stay here was just inside a fortnight, before the end of which we had got our new drafts allotted to their various companies; and a very good lot they were, though we feared they would have great difficulty in standing the heat if we were called upon to do long marches.

On 22nd March we started on our way to our first halting place El Burj. It was about nine miles, and we marched in the evenings, which was undoubtedly very wise. The going was not bad, there being a wire-netting track laid over all the softest parts: it is wonderful how satisfactory this is to march on, and many a time did we bless the man who invented it. The only sufferers were the mule leaders. They, naturally, could not lead their mules on the netting, and it was extra hard work for them, as they had to walk in the heavy sand and maintain the pace set by the troops who were on the good going. El Burj proved to be a most desolate spot, but it was at all events near wells; and we were so glad to hear that we were not to march straight on next day, that we didn't grumble much about the scenery.

The Higher Command were a little nervous that the Turks might slip away again as they had already done at El Arish; but the next few days were to show that this information was not correct, and that the Turk had no intention of leaving the Gaza-Beersheba line so long as he could hold on to it.

We stopped there four days, and marching once more in the evening, we did a comparatively short step to Sheikh Zowaid, camping about a mile short of the station. It was pitch dark when we arrived and we had no idea what our camp was like, and it was a great surprise to find in the morning that we were on the edge of a shallow salt lake. The sunrise on this sheet of water, fringed on the far side with a line of scattered palm trees, was really most exquisite. It was, however, the only good thing about the place. Water for breakfast was late in arriving, and we were told that the half-day's supply, which then arrived, had to fill the dixies for lunch, and also the water-bottles for the next march. There was not nearly enough for this, with the result that we had to start in the blazing sun about 1 P.M. with hardly anything in the bottles. The reason for this was, that the camels had to go on ahead to our next stop - Rafa - about thirteen miles distant, where it was hoped to have water drawn and ready for us on our arrival.

This afternoon march was a gruelling experience. It was the hottest part of the day; we had practically nothing in our water-bottles, and, to add to our trials, the wire-netting road was not laid beyond Sheikh Zowaid, as the ground had appeared quite firm to the divisions who had preceded us. Since they had passed, however, the route had been cut up by guns and transport, until it was just as soft as the softest sand, and twice as dusty. Finally, when we did get to Rafa about 7 P.M., there was no water waiting for us, and we found we had to take up an outpost line from the railway to the sea, a distance of about three miles, through the worst sandhills we had encountered. It was hopeless to move before the arrival of some water, and it was about 10 p.m. before we started to take up the line, and it was well after midnight before the left company had got the line extended right through to the shore. These sandhills were made of such fine sand that it was continuously blowing and drifting; any rifle pits dug out, say, a couple of feet, in the evening, would be completely obliterated in the morning.

Sending out supplies, as soon as it was light, to this distant company, was a most difficult job. To begin with, we found that camels, loaded with water fanatis, could not negotiate the steep faces of sand, so we had to do our best with the Lewis gun mules, carrying the fanatis only half full. Then there was a thick mist - the same mist which hampered the attack on Gaza - and we had no accurate knowledge of where the company was, nor was it possible to follow the tracks of the previous night, as they were all obliterated by the drifting sand. Luckily, some active members of the company had found the morning too cold for sitting still, and had taken a morning walk back from the line, so we came upon their fresh tracks, which led us to the rest of the company.

That night we had an alarm that the Turkish cavalry was out and had slipped round our right flank, and was likely to have a dash at our lines of communication either at Rafa or elsewhere, so we spent the night digging trenches which, during the next day or two, we improved into a sort of continuous line covering the water and railway station.

During these few days the first attack was made on Gaza, but without success. We heard a good many tales of hardship from lack of water, and saw some prisoners come through, but there was no great excitement.

From Rafa - which is on the Palestine Boundary - we moved on 30th March to Khan Yunis, said to be the home of Delilah. The march was once more in the evening, and was very comfortable, except for the last mile or two when we got in between the high hedges of prickly pear, and had to march through about a foot of dust in the most stifling atmosphere. When we arrived we found that we were once more on the fringes of civilisation: we could buy oranges in unlimited numbers, and also fresh eggs - not the Egyptian variety, about the size of a pigeon's egg, but real pukka hen's eggs. Water also was less scarce than it had been, and we were well content with our lot. We were in Brigade Reserve, which sounded very comfortable, but which was not so "cushy" as it sounded. It meant that we had to do all the unloading of supplies and ammunition at the supply depot and at the station, and also find the very large guards which were absolutely necessary, as the native was a diligent and skilful thief. The units in the outpost line really had much less to do, though, of course, they had their turns of night duty which we escaped.

Here we were joined by another brigade of our new division, and felt that at last we were about to become like other people - organised in a proper division.

This week, with its eggs and oranges, passed like a flash, and we once more moved on; this time quite a short way beyond Railhead at Deir-el-Belah, where we camped quite close to our compatriots the 52nd Division. After one night and a good bathe we took over, on 7th April, from the 54th Division a sector of trenches near Sheikh Nebhan, overlooking the hollow through which meandered the Wadi Ghuzzeh. This wadi - like all others in this part - is quite dry except during the storms of winter, but water could usually be got by sinking wells in the bed of the wadi at about ten or twelve feet down. Our cavalry by day and infantry by night held a line out beyond the wadi, covering the work of those who were sinking wells, making ramps for guns and transport crossings, and laying the water-pipe line. This line was to be carried to the cisterns of Um Gerrar, where it would come in very useful during the further operations for which we were preparing. It is rather wonderful to think that this water was carried with us by pipe line all the way from the Canal, and was actually Nile water brought to Kantara by the Sweetwater Canal.

The banks of the Wadi Ghuzzeh were almost everywhere precipitous, and anything from ten to twenty feet high. All these had to be ramped, and during the period of preparation some thirty such crossings were made between Tel-el-Jemmi and the sea, and each unit was allotted its crossing for the coming advance. During these days of preparation our Battalion dug a strong line of trenches dominating the crossings of the Wadi Ghuzzeh, and most of the officers got the chance of a reconnaissance to a distance of about three miles beyond the wadi.

The country beyond was very much cut up with smaller wadis, which at this time of year were a mass of wild flowers which grew most luxuriantly, and would have been welcome in most herbaceous borders; the anchusas - to name one - were several feet high, and covered with brilliant blue blooms, but the brightest effect was that of fields of mauve daisies. These grew as thick as poppies in Norfolk, and were almost as bright. One had plenty of time to look about at all the flowers, as there was practically no sign of a Turk, though, if one went too near up to the top of the watershed, an odd sniper would let off at one.

As the day for the advance drew near, all the troops told off for battle surplus were sent back to Railhead and formed into a divisional camp. Each battalion had to leave behind the following:- Either C.O. or 2nd in Command, two of the four Company Commanders and two of the four Company Sergeant-Majors, and a proportion of instructors in P.T., Lewis gun, musketry, gas, bombing, and signalling - in all, for a battalion at full strength, 120 of all ranks, including all officers above the number of 20.

This was the dustiest and dirtiest week of the whole year, the only interest being the scraps of gossip which kept coming in, and from which we pieced together the disastrous tale of the second battle of Gaza. One could also ride up to the top of Raspberry Hill or Im Seirat and see something for oneself, but usually any movement of troops was invisible owing to clouds of dust.

The fact that our main outpost line was, after this battle, advanced about live or six miles, was used to represent this battle as a British victory, but, as a matter of fact, it was a victory which failed to gain any main Turkish position. The positions which we held at the end of the battle, to which we had retired after being stopped at Ali-el-Muntar and Gaza itself, had been reached in the first instance with very few casualties, and it was on the glacis between these positions and the Turk that we suffered our main losses. This glacis was destitute of any cover, and was dominated by the heights of Ali-el-Muntar and the cactus hedges surrounding Gaza, and after many gallant efforts this had to be abandoned to form a No-Man's-Land of a mile or a mile and a half between ourselves and the Turk. On our left in the sandhills the progress was slower and steadier, and the line finished up a good deal nearer the Turk than on the right; but here again the cactus hedges lined with machine guns proved too much for us. Our Division was not used in this battle, being in reserve, which was lucky for us, as those who were in the front line of the attack all got a pretty severe knock.

On 19th April the Battalion left the outpost line on Sheikh Nebhan and marched towards Gaza, resting during the middle of the day on a ridge west of El Burjaliye, and moving in the afternoon on to Mansura Ridge in support. On the evening of 22nd April the Battalion moved forward to construct and occupy trenches at El Mendur, which was on the right, or refused, flank of the line, and there the details again joined us. There we had a good defensive position, but the trenches still had to be dug and, as luck would have it, this digging, which ought to have been nothing to our men fit as they were, in ordinary weather, was turned into a very high trial indeed by a khamsin. This red-hot and parching wind, blowing off the desert, makes thirst a positive torture when water is limited, and it was very limited at that time. We were getting rather less than half a gallon per man for all purposes, which is perhaps just about the quantity used by the ordinary man for cooking and drinking in the cold weather at home; but in a khamsin when you are doing five or six hours' hard manual labour per diem, a gallon is easily consumed. Luckily these heat waves only last about three days, but it left us pretty limp.

After a fortnight here a start was made with thinning out the line, in order to let some of those who had been engaged in the Gaza battle get a spell in reserve. We moved a step to our left, taking over with our Battalion the sector previously held by a brigade. Our portion of the line was taken over by the 12th (Ayr and Lanark Yeomanry) Battalion R.S.F., and we took over the line on the left previously held by the 5th and 7th Essex Regiments. Battalion H.Q. had a very comfortable pitch at the top of the Wadi Reuben, near a junction of many tracks which had been named Charing Cross.

Our week here meant another spell of steady work, as we had to convert what had previously been a continuous line into a series of strong posts, the intervals between which were covered by machine guns. This was known as the Dumb-bell Hill Sector of the Sheikh Abbas Line, being named from a hill whose contours on the map were a very fair imitation of a dumb-bell. Here we were still facing to a flank, but our left came up to the corner where the proper front began, which meant that we lay enfiladed from the main front, and they used to throw over a good deal of stuff if ever they spotted any movement.

At the beginning of May we did another move, this time on to the real front in the Sheikh Abbas Sector. This was quite a pleasant place, as we lived on the reverse slope of a fairly steep bank, pretty well defiladed from all the Turk guns, and the trenches, though only

DUG-OUTS IN THE FRONT LINE. SHEIKH ABBAS.

A RESERVE WADI, SHEIKH ABBAS.

in most places a single line with quite insufficient communication trenches, had a long view and a good field of fire. The wire was continuous though not very thick, and it was quite safe to leave the trenches during the day in charge of a few observation posts. Add to this the fact that all, except the posts, could walk about during the day in the open quite covered from view by the steep slope mentioned above, consequently it was trench warfare under the most pleasant possible conditions. All the same it was a trying life owing to the difficulty of getting a normal amount of sleep. We had to "stand to" from about 3 A.M. till dawn, and then work till breakfast, and on to about 9.30 A.M. By that time it was too hot to do any more, and the rest of the day had to be spent in idleness. Few of us could sleep during the day because of the heat, and the temperature seldom began to get much cooler before 8.30 P.M., and sometimes later. There was nothing doing in the way of warfare beyond continuous patrols at night, sometimes small, sometimes up to twenty or more. The only occasion during our first stay did anything in the nature of a skirmish take place, and that was brought on by one of our patrols having a narrow escape of being cut off at dawn near a place called Two Tree Farm. One of the platoons in the line saw what was happening and went out to support them, and managed to get them in all right. A very small affair, but quite exciting for the onlookers, when there is nothing more important doing. In this part there was about a mile of No-Man's-Land, and the Turk was very completely wired in and was seldom to be found outside his wire. Most of our patrols in consequence came in without having seen a Turk at all, but it was not a comfortable job, as machine guns were firing bursts all night.

We had a fortnight in the line, and on 25th May came out to Brigade Reserve which was only a move of a couple of hundred yards and not half so comfortable; but it gave some of us the opportunity of riding over towards the sea and having a look at our own and the Turkish lines on the sandhills.

While we were here we marched to Deir-el-Belah to be disinfected, and later relieved, first, the 16th (Royal 1st Devon Yeomanry) Devonshire Regiment, and then the Ayr and Lanarks, to allow them to do the same. On 13th June we took over the centre sector, the Abbas Apex Sector, of the Brigade line from the Devons, and remained in the line till 9th July when we handed over to the 4th Royal Scots, 52nd Division. Every night we sent out a patrol of 1 N.C.O. and 10 men, either as a standing patrol on Essex Hill or to patrol the wire in front of our area, and an officer's patrol consisting of an officer and 20 men to cover the ground between Two Tree Farm and Old British Trenches. These patrols were nearly always fired on, but we were in luck's way as regards casualties.

We then marched back some four miles to the Dorset House area, where we at once got started on intensive training for open warfare, varied with some very hurried musketry in the Wadi Ghuzzeh. Whilst here we had a very thorough inspection by Lieut.-General Sir P.W. Chetwode, K.C.M.G., C.B., D.S.O., Commanding Eastern Force, and in the way of amusements managed to get one or two games of polo with a neighbouring brigade. The plain on which we played was in full view of some of the Turkish positions at Gaza, and on one or two occasions play was stopped by shells. Also, in rotation by battalions, we made bathing expeditions to the sea at Regent's Park. It was seven miles each way, but was well worth the trouble as it was months since most of us had been in the sea.

At the beginning of August we again changed our camp, and while on the move put in a couple of days' field firing. For once in a way the ground lent itself to the purpose, and we had most interesting days; but it was pretty warm work, not being confined to morning and evening. Our new camp was right in the sandhills, near the aerodrome at Deir-el-Belah, where we did intensive divisional training. This was to have lasted three weeks, and was a very strenuous business. A full divisional day meant leaving camp any time after 2 A.M. and not getting back again until after midday; it was usually interesting for the senior ranks, but intensely boring for everyone else. Luckily we were able to fit in bathing, concerts, and sports, which kept everyone cheery.

After a fortnight of this we found we were at last told off for a useful job of work - digging a new line of trenches in the sandhills facing Gaza, between Fusilier Ridge and Jones' Post, in front of those on Samson's and Fusilier's Ridges, at that time held by the 54th Division. We moved over the Wadi Ghuzzeh to Regent's Park, where we camped right on the shore about an hour and a half's march from the scene of our labours. After the second night it was decided that this was too remote, and we moved up nearer our work. Here we stayed for a week, with half of each battalion digging each night. It was a tiresome job, as the sand was so soft that a very wide ditch had to be dug and then faced with sandbags. The men were very quick about getting down, and after the first night they were practically working in safety for the remaining four or five days necessary to complete the sandbag revetting. All bags used had to be double, as single ones would not keep the sand in.

Our first night was a pretty jumpy business. We were somewhere about 500 yards from the Turk lines, and there was a bright moon, with the result that he spotted something and gave us quite a bombardment. For some time there was considerable doubt whether the work should be attempted at all, but thanks largely to Lieut.-Colonel J. Gilmour, who subsequently got a D.S.O. for his work that night, a good start was made at the cost of a few casualties. The rest of the week passed quietly, but we were quite glad at the end of it to be relieved by a battalion of the Norfolk Regiment of another brigade, as the march both ways, plus digging, was very hard work.

We did not return to the camp we had left, but to the Wadi Selke, a mile or two inland from Deir-el-Belah. The distance from

A PLATOON MESS, WADI ASHER.

"C" COMPANY OFFICERS' MESS, WADI ASHER.

the sea made bathing a bit of a toil, but otherwise it was a good camp, especially for the officers, whose bivouacs were in a fig grove which bore a very heavy crop of excellent figs. We stayed here about seven weeks, the longest spell we had in any one place, and made it into a good camp. There was a fair football ground on which we got through an inter-platoon American tournament, which kept everybody amused. There used to be a great turn-out when the officers' team was due to play - they occasionally won their matches. We also had a good 200 yards' range with sixteen targets, and carried out innumerable experiments to decide upon the best methods of attack. We had exhibitions of wire-cutting and smoke screens, bangalore torpedoes, and many days of practising co-operation with aeroplanes. Very frequent night marches by compass, combined with digging in, and followed by an attack or advance at dawn. In fact, we were put through a very practical training for the task which we were later to undertake.

In order to minimise the chance of anything going wrong with the plans for the concentration and attack on Beersheba, many officers were given the chance of making a reconnaissance as near as possible to the Turkish positions. This was done from Gamli, a place on the Wadi Ghuzzeh about fifteen miles inland and about eleven from us. We rode over there the night before, and in the early morning the cavalry moved out and pushed their line within a mile or two of the Beersheba defences. Covered by this, parties of officers rode out and familiarised themselves with the sector in which their unit was to operate, and they were thus able to hand in reports upon which Brigade Staffs could allot concentration areas and routes.

At the moment of kicking off we were as well trained as we were ever likely to be, and, what is more important, were very fit and full of the offensive spirit. The concentration started on 25th October, when we marched some six miles to Abu Sitta. Our transport establishment had been very carefully thought out, and, though both animals and vehicles were undoubtedly overloaded at the start, this soon rectified itself, as consumable stores could not be replaced. We had one camel per battalion for officers' mess, and he started out very fully laden. He was a good deal less heavily loaded towards the end of the operations. Next day we marched on beyond the Wadi at Gamli - a very dusty and tiresome march - and were to have remained there throughout the next day. Word came in, however, that the Turk was attacking our outpost line at El Buggar, some ten miles out, and the Battalion had to move off at a moment's notice about noon. The march through the heat of the afternoon was most trying, and on arrival it was found the enemy were occupying part of the line we were to take up. They withdrew, however, in the evening, and we constructed a series of strong posts from the Beersheba road to south of El Buggar.

During these days of concentration the plain lying between Shellal and Beersheba had been the scene of great activities. Karm had been selected as the position for a forward supply dump, and both light and broad gauge railways were being pushed out towards it at top speed. The first blow of the campaign was to be launched at the defences of Beersheba, which were facing west and extended both north and south of the Wadi Saba. They occupied a commanding position and were continuously wired. The main attack was to be pushed home south of the Wadi Saba by the 74th and 60th Divisions, and at the same time the enemy's extreme left flank was to be turned by the cavalry, who were to make a wide detour through very difficult and waterless country and attack Beersheba from the east, and, if possible, cut off the retreat of the garrison of the Beersheba area. Covering all these preparations an outpost line was established some miles east of Karm and El Buggar, held on the left by the 53rd Division, then the 74th Division, then the Imperial Camel Corps, and, south of the Wadi Saba, where it was much more lightly held, a mere line of cavalry observation posts. These cavalry posts were covering, and slightly in advance of, the positions selected for battle headquarters for the 74th and 60th Divisions.

The preliminary arrangements for the troop movements went like clockwork, as did also the approach marches to the positions of deployment, and at the appointed time on 30th October, the Divisional H.Q. moved up the five or six miles to the battle stations selected. There was no sign of crowding or confusion - the only indication that there was anything unusual on, was the dust which could be seen here and there. The moves of the infantry began just as it was getting dusk, and long before dawn both the 60th and 74th Divisions had their two brigades on the line of deployment, which stretched southwards some three or four miles from the Wadi Saba.

As soon as it was daylight a bombardment of the Turkish advanced position on Hill 1070 was started, smothering the entire landscape in clouds of dust. This first attack, which was carried through by one of the brigades of the 60th Division, was ordered at 8.30 A.M. Hill 1070 was carried at 8.45, and during the next hour all the remaining advanced positions fell, and it was even reported that the enemy was here and there evacuating portions of his main line. There was now another interval for bombardment, whilst the gunners were wire-cutting for the attack on the main positions. During this period of waiting, which was longer than had been expected, our infantry suffered a good deal from shelling, much of which was in enfilade from positions north of the Wadi, and it was with relief that they received the order about 12.15 to proceed with the main attack. In about forty minutes all the trenches opposite the 60th Division were captured, and the 74th completed their task only about twenty minutes later, one brigade having had some difficulty owing to incomplete wire-cutting. The 60th had, by 2 P.M., advanced some way beyond the captured trenches towards Beersheba, and the 74th crossed the Wadi Saba and cleared the trenches northward to the barrier on the Fara-Beersheba road.

TURKISH TRENCH WITH DEAD TURKS.
HILL 1070, NEAR BEERSHEBA.

BATHING, REGENT'S PARK.

Meantime the cavalry had found their detour even lengthier than had been expected, with the result that they were some hours later than they should have been, and were held up for most of the day by trenches at Tel-el-Saba, a mile or more east of Beersheba proper. These were, however, rushed towards evening, and Beersheba was occupied that night. Very few of the troops allotted for the defence of Beersheba escaped, the whole operation being completely successful. The Engineers at first reported that the water supply and wells were intact; but this proved to be far from the fact, and within forty-eight hours the shortage of water was being severely felt. After this smashing success in the first stage of operations all our tails were well up, and everyone was keen to know what was to be the next move.

The next day found the 60th concentrated at Beersheba; the 74th just north of the barrier on the Fara-Beersheba road, while an advance northward had been begun by the 53rd and, in the evening, by a party of the 74th. One brigade group for the former advanced in a northerly direction west of Ain Kohleh, and the remainder in a north-westerly direction on Kuweilfeh. The left advance was successful, and a line was established on the desired objective, a ridge running east and west some five or six miles north of Beersheba. The other advance was not so fortunate; something went wrong with the supplies both of water and ammunition, and strong opposition was encountered. Also, it was impossible country to campaign in; practically roadless, and very much broken up with wadis and rocky precipices, which made it most difficult to maintain communications, even though a mounted brigade was thrown in to help.

The situation up here was much the same next day. No great progress had been made, nor were good communications established, but they had managed to get through both water and ammunition. Other divisions were, however, kept on the move. The 74th were moved up to take over some line from the left of the 53rd, the 60th were concentrated some three miles N.W. of Beersheba, and one brigade of the 10th was moved to Irgeig. This was an anxious day, as the 53rd seemed to be quite held up at Kuweilfeh and not too well provided with supplies, and there was considerable doubt, in view of the general scarcity of water, whether it would be possible to carry on the campaign, which involved rolling up the Sheria and Kuwauka defences from the east.

Our Intelligence Department had for the moment "lost" a Turkish division, which complicated the situation very much as, if it were suddenly to appear on the right flank of our attack on Sheria, a most serious situation would be created. However, on the afternoon of the 5th, word was received from the 53rd Division that they had captured prisoners from numerous different battalions, some of which were known to belong to the missing division. This settled the question, as it was quite clear that the 53rd were keeping them too busy at Kuweilfeh for them to be able to send any serious force to Sheria. The "lost" division it seems was one which had been sent to reinforce the forces defending Beersheba, but by the time it got to Sheria the Beersheba defences were taken, and it was obviously no use going there. It was accordingly then sent to Kuweilfeh in anticipation of an attempt by us to turn their extreme left flank.

On the afternoon of the 5th orders were rapidly issued for the attack next day on the Sheria defences and the Kuwauka system.

As most of the troops destined for the Sheria attack were at this time in the outpost line, this meant a concentration and deployment by night in an unknown country where map reading was very difficult indeed, and it was most creditable that it should have been, as it was, successfully carried out. There were certain minor mistakes, but in the main the attack came off as planned, and by midday all the line of the Sheria defences were in our hands.

The spearhead of the attack was the 229th Brigade, with ourselves and the Somersets in the front line, and it was a brilliant affair from start to finish. The brigades on our right and left, the 230th Brigade and a brigade of the 60th Division, were echelonned in rear of us, and the prompt success of our attack greatly assisted the advance of the 60th and 10th Divisions on the Kuwauka system. Our Lewis guns especially gave great assistance, and were successful in preventing the Turks from removing several of their guns, placed in rear of the Kuwauka system. This was acknowledged by the 60th Division who, in the true sporting spirit, let our Division know that they did not claim those guns as captured by them, though it was by their men that the guns were actually collected.

The guns of the 60th and 10th Divisions served them well and cut the wire most thoroughly and, without any undue number of casualties, the positions were finally taken about 2.30 P.M. The 10th then took over the line from the 60th, who advanced to the attack on the wells and railway station at Tel-el-Sheria. Unfortunately it was by this time getting dark, and direction was to some extent lost. The Turk put up a good fight here, and it was not until the morning that the wells and station were in our hands. We could see their dumps blazing all night far to the north, and it was clear that they had made up their minds to a general retreat.

These first six days in November had been strenuous days for the Battalion. On 30th October the Corps Cavalry and I.C.C. had passed through our lines, and we moved up to a position in Dundee Wadi. The 231st Brigade then passed through and took over from us, attacking along with 230th Brigade working in conjunction with the 60th and Cavalry Divisions. On 2nd November we took over the outpost line from the 2/10th Middlesex Regiment (53rd Division), and on 4th November we again advanced our line, meeting with no opposition except sniping and intermittent shell fire. At 7 P.M. on the evening of 5th November we received orders for the attack on the enemy's position, were relieved at 9 P.M. by a battalion of the 230th Brigade, and at 11 P.M. moved off to the point of deployment.

At 3.30 on the morning of 6th November we deployed for the attack, the 230th Brigade being on our right, and the Somersets on our left. The advance began at five and we were badly enfiladed from the right where the attacking troops were being held up, and whence we continued to be enfiladed until we detached a couple of platoons, who carried the enemy's positions there by 6.15. By 5.55 we had taken our first objective and captured four guns, all limbered up and trying to get away. We promptly attacked the ridge beyond, and having captured it proceeded to consolidate. At midday we again advanced under pretty heavy fire, but the Lewis gunners were very well handled, and succeeded in knocking out the crew and teams of two field guns beyond the railway, and we carried on to the position just east of the railway.

Our casualties at the Battle of Sheria were Major G.E.B. Osborne, Lieutenants J.D. Kinniburgh and E.A. Thompson, and 47 other ranks killed, and 5 officers and 182 other ranks wounded, of whom 13 subsequently died in hospital. Among the wounded was Lieut.-Colonel J. Gilmour, who was hit at the very end of the day, and to whom was due no small part of the credit for the victory. His brilliant leadership and dash at Sheria earned him a well-won bar to his D.S.O., and the admiration of the whole Brigade. The elan and dash of the Battalion, under his inspiring leadership, throughout the operations gained the highest praise from all quarters. Between 5 A.M. and midday the Battalion along with the Somersets had advanced some 10,000 yards, in the course of which they had captured several successive all-round positions held by considerable garrisons, and well provided with machine guns. In addition to 99 prisoners we had captured six field guns with limbers, three machine guns, and a large quantity of S.A.A. Our dead were buried in the cactus garden.

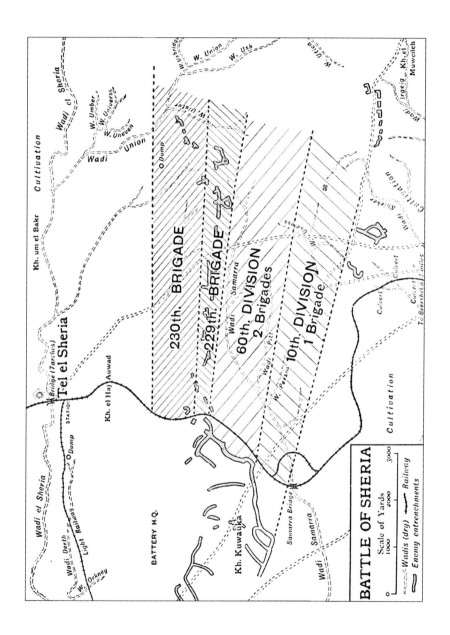

BATTLE OF SHERIA

Scale of Yards
0   1000   2000   3000

--- Wadis (dry)   —→— Railway
Enemy entrenchments

Major J. Younger who had been acting as liason-officer between the 60th and 74th Divisions was sent for to take over command of the Battalion, which was in the highest of spirits in spite of all it had come through, full of beans, very proud of themselves and the Colonel, and more than ready for another scrap.

We were all thoroughly glad to have had such a good introduction to infantry work; not only had it been a success, but it had also been well planned. The staff work had been excellent and, above all, it had been open warfare for which we thought, rightly or wrongly, that our mounted training had prepared us.

We had now got some news of the doings of the other corps on the coast. We knew that they had succeeded in taking Gaza and were advancing north, and we saw the cavalry divisions galloping through us brigade after brigade to take up the pursuit. The Turk was in a most awkward position, but proved himself a first-class rear-guard fighter.

On the night of the 7th he had only the narrow neck between the cavalry and the XXI. Corps, who were advancing up the coast, and this neck was not more than five or six miles wide; but in spite of all difficulties he managed to get most of his infantry and some of his guns away. We ourselves expected to start our advance north following on the cavalry, but it turned out that the transport was not able to maintain two corps so far in advance of Railhead. The XXI. Corps, being already on its way north, was given the task of clearing the Plain of Philistia, and following up the Turkish retreat with the assistance of a considerable portion of our (XX. Corps) transport. As we were not to go on, the authorities were in no hurry to move us, and we spent a couple of days clearing up the battlefield before returning in a couple of the dustiest and most unpleasant marches to the neighbourhood of Karm.

Our actual destination was Goz-el-Gelieb; but when we got near the spot it was so thick with dust that we could only see about 50 yards, and as the plain was quite featureless and all alike, we just bivouacked for the night, and hoped we should find in the morning that we were somewhere near the right spot.

First thing after daylight, while the dew was still able to keep down the dust, we got our bearings and moved about three-quarters of a mile to the correct map reference. Here we were joined during the day by our "B" team or battle surplus, whom we had last seen a fortnight before, and a draft of 2 officers and 126 other ranks out from home.

On 15th November Major-General E. S. Girdwood, commanding 74th Division, at a Brigade Parade presented Military Medals, awarded for gallantry at the Battle of Sheria, when 9 men from the Battalion received the honour.

After a few days in the dust of this plain, we moved back in two marches to our old area near the coast. This time we were just south of the Wadi Ghuzzeh, on a hill which was beautifully green and fresh. All the lower ground round it had been used for camps for the best part of a year, but this hill had been so prominent and so fully under observation from Ali-el-Muntar, that it could not be occupied so long as the Turks held Gaza. Here we had a great presentation of medals by the Corps Commander (Lieut.-General Sir Philip W. Chetwode, commanding XX. Corps). Our share for Sheria was 1 D.S.O., 4 M.C., 5 D.C.M., and 1 more M.M. making 10 M.M. in all, which we all agreed was a quite satisfactory allowance. Evidently the authorities at home thought so, if one may judge from the fact that there was practically nothing obtainable for the next six months.

We were told by the authorities that we were certain to remain some time in the Gaza area, where we were fully occupied in salvage work, for the simple reason that the Q Branch could not feed us if we moved beyond Railhead. Some new factor must, however, have arisen, as we had only stayed some five days, and most of the Battalion was out some four or five miles away on salvage work, when suddenly orders arrived that we were to march that afternoon. - Starting point, the crossing of the Wadi Guzzeh, 4.30 P.M.

Before describing our march it would be as well to give some idea of the position of the XXI. Corps, which had been, with the assistance of the cavalry, pushing the Turkish forces back on to Jerusalem and Jaffa. This pursuit, which met with a pretty stout resistance throughout, had been going on for nearly a fortnight, and the Plain of Philistia was cleared of the Turk, whose main forces had retired on our left a little beyond Jaffa, and on our right into the precipitous Judæan Highlands defending Jerusalem. Our Railhead had only reached Deir Sineid, a few miles north of Gaza, and about thirty-five miles south of the battle front. The Turkish railway, which went as far as Junction Station, and from which much had been hoped, proved almost useless owing to shortage of rolling stock, and consequently supply depended almost entirely on motor lorry and camel from Railhead, or from the Wadi Sukharieh, where some supplies were being landed in surf boats. The question of supply had been most difficult, and water supply hardly less so, even for the one corps, and it looked as if we might come in for some scarcity when we got up nearer the front. In the pursuit of the portion of the Turkish Army, which was retiring on Jerusalem, our cavalry had penetrated some way into the hills, and were endeavouring to hold on until the infantry could get up to relieve them. The process of relief was going on during the few days we were marching up.

Now to return to our part in the affair. Our first march was a short one of some seven or eight miles to a bivouac a mile beyond Ali-el-Muntar, the prominent height dominating Gaza at which we had been looking the whole summer. We stayed here for a day, partly to wait for the arrival of greatcoats, which would be so necessary in the Judæan Highlands, and to get rid of our helmets, and partly to give the supply people a chance. Most of us spent an hour or two examining Ali-el-Muntar and its defences. It looked very much less knocked about than one would have expected after the severe bombardments to which it had been subjected, and we came to the conclusion that there had never been very many troops actually holding it. The infantry had evidently been in trenches well away from the hill, which appeared to have been used entirely for observation purposes. It must have been a pretty uncomfortable corner for an F.O.O., as the top used to appear to be blown off about three times a day. Concealment of trenches had been made very easy by the presence of numerous cactus hedges, and it is doubtful whether our guns, except in the actual assault, had ever had a really satisfactory target.

After this day of rest, 24th November, we marched just over twelve miles to Mejdal. The weather was not too hot, and there was quite a good beaten mud road, and we should have found it a fairly easy march if it had not been for foot troubles. We had been more than six months without having ever marched on a road - it had usually been soft sand - and the sudden change to the flat hard surface of the baked mud fired the men's feet at once. When we arrived in camp at Mejdal we had a foot parade, and found that there were over a hundred cases of blisters and dressings for the medical officer and his satellites. This Mejdal was quite a considerable village, and as we marched in we met the most dignified specimens of native we had yet seen. Mounted on donkeys and wearing the flowing robes of the Old Testament, they really did remind one of the patriarchs in our stained glass windows. All the brilliant colours - purple, crimson, and orange - were represented, and many of them had the regulation beard. There were also numbers of the usual class selling oranges and, oddly enough, also cigarettes.

Next morning we were again on the road and not feeling too cheery about it, as we were told we were to do a 19-mile march - rather a formidable proposition when every second man already had sore feet - as it was the intention of the authorities to get us up to Jaffa in two strenuous marches. However, during the course of the day the plan of campaign was changed, and we were told that we should probably have to go to the Judæan Hills instead of to the Ramleh-Jaffa Sector near the sea. This was not the best of news, as there was no doubt which was the more salubrious spot; but it had this compensation that it knocked six miles off our day's march, our camp being pitched near the Wadi Sukharieh mentioned above, which was a convenient starting-point for the next day whether we were ordered to Ramleh or to Junction Station. We found, to our surprise, that the feet were no worse than the previous night; some few were getting pretty bad, but most of them looked as if they were on the mend.

The next day we were finally labelled Judæa, and did a most trying march - only about eleven miles, but a frightfully hot day - at first through various pleasant looking farm colonies, and later through a most desolate piece of country to Junction Station. On this trek we were lucky enough to come under the eye of the Commander-in-Chief, who at once noticed what we all very well knew - that we were carrying a much greater load than could reasonably be expected in such a climate. We had to do it, as the necessary camels had simply not been available. However, the Commander-in-Chief quickly remedied this, and from here onwards we had camels provided to carry our greatcoats, leaving us pack and blanket only.

At Junction Station we had our first taste of water trouble. As we were making our way from west to east, we were changing places with a division of the XXI. Corps. This division had spent the previous night at Junction Station and had drunk the wells dry, so that no water was obtainable on our arrival. We were told we should get it by 9 P.M., and then a later hour was mentioned; but the net result was that we got just enough to make our breakfast tea, but not enough to fill the water-bottles, so we started on our next stage in the very worst of tempers to find that we had hardly got out of camp before we were involved in a regular block at the railway crossing which, needless to say, was frightfully dusty. This delay proved, however, to be a blessing in disguise, as it enabled our water camels to catch us up with a small ration of water for lunch. If we had not got this water we should probably not have got more than 75 per cent. of the Brigade to the end of the day's journey. We got into camp on a rocky slope near Latron about dusk, and almost at once were warned to be ready to start again at 9 P.M. to march another ten miles and take over part of the line in the hills. This was soon altered to starting at 3 A.M. owing to better news from the front, and again to 8 A.M. the next morning as the situation calmed down.

It was now becoming really interesting, as we expected to be in the line within twenty-four hours, and all sorts of rumours were current. Generally it was understood that we had penetrated successfully into the hills until we were brought to a halt by the difficulties of supply, and that now the Turk was beginning to recover from the effects of his long retreat and was launching counter-attacks, which had in some cases been fairly successful, and that he had given the XXI. Corps a couple of heavy knocks to the north-west of Jerusalem. It was expected that the XXI. Corps would be pulled out to the comparative comfort of the Coastal Sector, while we - the XX. Corps - were to have the honour of attacking, and we hoped, capturing Jerusalem.

We had now been marching for six days and most of us found our feet improving and getting accustomed to the roads, though we had lost some twenty-five good men, who had kept going like good 'uns with really sore feet until they had to be sent to hospital by the M.O. That is one great joy about the British Tommy, if things are really "business" he will stick almost anything. Men who had protested before and during every route march in training that they could not carry a pack more than a few miles, and who literally had to be hunted home, did all these marches up to the front without faltering, though they were incomparably harder and though a heavier load was being carried.

Our next march was a short one of six miles into the foothills to Beit Sirra, a spot quite close to Likia, in a piece of country we were to know very thoroughly before we were done. Here we spent an uneasy night "in readiness to move"; but it was not till next morning that we really took to the hills, marching up a most precipitous Roman road to a spot which can only be described as Q 20, central. It was close to the Roman road and about half-way between Likia and Kubeibe, and lay on the covered side of the ridge south of that on which our line was at that time established.

Next day we got orders to take over a bit of the line, and towards evening we climbed down into the Wadi Selman, and up the other side to relieve another brigade of our Division. This turned out to be a pretty jumpy business, as there had been some heavy fighting on our right during the afternoon, and the people we relieved told us that, to our right, all the ridge north of the Wadi Selman was in the hands of the Turks, and that they might be expected to advance at any time against our right flank, and that they themselves, though they had not got it definitely, understood that our line was to be withdrawn behind the Wadi Selman.

The sector which we were supposed to take over extended from Hill 1750 - where, presumably, even if we ever had had touch with our own troops, our flank would now be right in the air - to the Wadi Zait. A deep and precipitous wadi - the Shebab - ran from the Turkish positions through the centre of our sector down to our Battalion H.Q. in the Wadi Selman. We had no news of any change in the situation on our left, so assumed it must be all right, and one company was sent up the hill to occupy the portion of the line to the left (or west) of the Wadi Shebab, getting touch with the 52nd Division on their extreme left. This lot were lucky enough to find an enamelled wire already laid from Battalion H.Q. to their Company H.Q. and, though it was broken in one or two places by mules during the relief, they soon got it patched up and in communication with Battalion H.Q. A company and a half was sent to the right of the Wadi Shebab to move in fighting order towards Hill 1750, making good the ridge as they proceeded. There was no chance of getting wire out here, nor had we enough lamps to establish a transmitting station, which was necessary; but by using our own Orilux torches we managed to get through one or two brief reports of progress, and at last, about 2 A.M., a message came through that they thought they were on the hill and had encountered no opposition.

In the morning as soon as it was light, Lieut.-Colonel Younger started out to see the right flank, and soon decided that they were not on Hill 1750, which he made out to be twin knolls some half a mile further on, and just about the same height as the hill we were occupying. On one of these peaks we thought we saw a few Turks, and about midday D Company (Captain H.S. Sharp) made a detour down half-way to the Wadi Selman in our rear, and then advanced straight up the cliff at these two peaks. They got to the top unopposed, but the moment they showed over the skyline they were met with a hail of machine-gun bullets and shrapnel, the position being completely dominated by the Turks at medium range. How it was no one could understand, but the attackers only had one casualty on the top, and he was very gallantly brought back by the officer in charge of the company. We stuck to one twin peak but evacuated the other, and it was now clear that 1750 was still farther on, and that the Turk was occupying it, so that, in order to have a dash at it, the first thing to do was to extend our line farther to the right and get in touch with some of our own troops. Distances and contours were almost impossible to appreciate from the map, and it was not realised what a great extent of line we were being asked to hold with a battalion, and really, faulty map reading was excusable, considering the maps we had to work with.

To begin with, the map was two miles to the inch, and was not contoured - merely hachured - which is no earthly use where the peaks are crowded up within a few hundred yards of each other, so that three peaks in line appear on the map as one ridge, though there may be dips of 500 feet between them, and looking at it the other way, it is very hard to believe that a place which it takes you one and a half hours to reach walking is less than a mile on the map. We were all deceived, but by good luck on this occasion no harm was done.

Brigade at once sent up three companies and some machine-gunners to support us, so we were all right in the line; but they proved to be too many for the signal communications, which all had to come through Battalion H.Q., and the signallers were worked to death. All these odd companies and the machine-gunners had to arrange for their own supply of ammunition, water, and rations with their own units, as they were the only people who could supply the necessary pack animals to bring the stuff as far as Battalion H.Q. From here the stores had to be carried by hand by fatigue parties, and these parties had to be advised by signals whenever their stores arrived. This meant continuous work for the signallers, who had to keep their stations going with insufficient reliefs, a thing that can only be done for a very limited time.

We had hardly got this extended disposition complete when orders were received to relieve two companies of the Devons, as their battalion was down to carry out an attack that night. Of course as luck would have it, the companies were right up on the top of the hill, and the only people available to relieve them were the companies which had just come down after having done a couple of days up there. However, there was nothing else for it, and they just had to go back, with the promise that they would be relieved as soon as Brigade sent the troops to replace them. During the afternoon the senior officers from the attacking battalion came down to reconnoitre, but it was about 4 P.M. by the time they got down, and consequently they had only time to see their objective from one point of view which, as it happened, was a fatal misfortune, as it left them with quite a false impression of what their position would be when once they got their objective. There was some discussion as to whether it should be a raid or a consolidation. All those on the spot favoured a raid, but judging from the map it appeared a desirable position to consolidate, and this was finally ordered.

Almost every division made one such mistake when first operating in this mountainous country, and this was to prove to be ours. The objective was the hill and village of Beit-ur-el-Foka - the Upper Bethhoron of the Bible, where the sun stood still for Joshua - which seemed to occupy a commanding position on the old Roman road between Beit-ur-el-Tahta and El Jib, and was marked clearly on the map. It was also supposed to contain water, and to be desirable for that reason. The attack was carried out by an advance up the Wadi Zait to a position of deployment at the foot of Foka Hill itself, whence the summit was successfully rushed. There were few casualties and a good haul of prisoners - somewhere about 150. But it was to prove impossible to remain there. The position itself was not sufficiently roomy for a battalion, and no digging was possible owing to the rocky ground. It was also too exposed from no less than three sides.

Opposite, across the Wadi Imaish, which ran east and west, roughly N.N.E. from Foka, was the dominating ridge of Zeitun, some hundreds of feet higher than Foka and under 1800 yards away; to the N.N.W., perhaps 2000 yards off, was the crest of Khirbet Kereina, fully as high as Foka; and, as if these two dominating positions in front, giving first-class artillery observation, were not enough, there was also a hill, subsequently known as Hill A, which was just about the same height as Foka, was held by some Turks with one or two machine guns, and fired slap into their right rear from the south-east. This last was only some 500 or 600 yards away, but was divided from Foka by a deep ravine, and it was found impossible to send a detachment to storm it. It was this hill in rear that sealed the doom of the business. They might have managed to stick it out in spite of the rifle and artillery fire in front until the Turks got tired of it, but the fire from the rear limited all movement and all getting up of bombs and ammunition. Under cover of rifle fire and shrapnel the Turks stormed up again and again, climbing up the steep face of the Wadi Imaish where our guns could not have touched them, even if they had had - which they hadn't - any decent arrangements for observation. Once up within bombing distance, the Turk had the great advantage of a large supply of bombs, whereas we had not had time to get up more than a few which were soon exhausted. Even ammunition was not too plentiful, as everything had to be carried up the very steep Wadi Zait, the top portion of which was commanded from Hill A. The best way for evacuating wounded proved to be down the Roman road to Beit-ur-el-Tahta, where they were handed over to the 10th Division who were now on our left.

To make a long story short, the O.C. Battalion had to make up his mind to quit, and he had a hard job, even with some assistance from the 10th Division on Tahta Ridge, to bring away his wounded who were very numerous. About 3 p.m. the last of them came out, having had a terrible day, only four or five officers remaining unwounded. They stuck to it well, but it was an untenable position. The Turk contented himself with driving them off the Foka Heights, and did not attempt to advance farther - if he had, it might have proved just as bad for him as Foka had been for us.

On 4th December we were relieved by the 6th Munster Regiment and went back to our old camp at Q 20 central, where our transport had remained all the time. Here we rested for a couple of days. We found that our Division had been pulled out, in order to take part in the sweeping movement by which it was hoped to capture Jerusalem. On the third day after our relief we moved out, in floods of rain, along the so-called road to Kubeibe, where, along with the battalion which had been in Foka and half the machine-gun company, we were to form the Divisional Reserve for the first phase of the operations. It was an awful night, and the track was so steep and slippery that the camels could not get on, and there was broken-down transport every few hundred yards along the track which was charitably described on the map as a road. The site of our bivouac was partly rocky ledges and partly slippery mud, and we spent a most uncomfortable night. The attacking troops of the Division moved to their positions of deployment the same night, and in the early morning successfully took the Beit Iksa trenches, which were the first objective. The next stage - the capture of the El Burj Ridge and Neby Samwil - was not so rapid, but all were in our hands on the following day (8th December) and, on our right, the 60th Division had made equally good progress in face of determined opposition south of the Jaffa-Jerusalem road.

On 8th December 3 officers and 100 other ranks went off road-making. One officer and 30 other ranks formed a military cordon round Kubeibeh, and 1 officer and 50 men proceeded to Enab to represent Scotland in the Guard of Honour which it was hoped would be required for the entry into Jerusalem. Thirty more for A.S.C. fatigues at Kuryet-el-Enab, and another lot to fetch from Latron a lot of donkeys, which were to be added to our transport establishment. The result was that, when about 5 P.M. we were ordered to rejoin the Brigade in the neighbourhood of Beit Iksa, we could only muster about 200 of all ranks. The Senior Company Commander was accordingly left behind to collect what he could and follow on, and we started off with the rest of the Divisional Reserve to do the six or seven miles in the dark in single file. We could not use the road - so-called - from Kubeibe to Beit Iksa, as we could not discover whether the village was wholly in our hands, so we wandered on in pitch darkness with no path of any kind to show us the best way along the most precipitous slopes, and the most dangerous wadis. The camels were entirely unable to follow, and even the mules were in difficulties, several of them falling over ledges and down terraces. It was 1 A.M. (we started about 5 P.M.) before we reached the locality in which we had expected to find the Brigade, but we could find no trace of them, and there was nothing to be done but send out a few scouts to look for them, and lie down and sleep until daylight.

The situation was not improved by the fact that all ration convoys had broken down the day before owing to the slippery tracks, and we had only the unexpired portion (*i.e.*, breakfast) instead of two days' ration plus the unexpired portion as we should have had, and as the authorities no doubt thought we had. We had also no confidence that those who were responsible for bringing up the overdue rations had any idea where to look for us even if the weather improved sufficiently to allow them to make use of the tracks. We understood that we were in for a four days' push, and it looked like being a real hungry one. This proved to be the case, as no rations reached us until the end of the operations; but luckily they lasted only two days instead of four.

Next morning, the 9th, just before dawn, someone came rattling down the steep slope above us, and to our joy we found it was the Brigade-Major coming to look for us, and that Brigade H.Q. was just above us - "just above" being 600 feet up one of the steepest slopes one could climb. However, we got up all right about 7 A.M. and managed to get a bit of our precious food disposed of before we received orders to move.

Our part in the assault of Jerusalem was to march with all speed to take up a position on Tel-el-Ful, a hill some 2500 feet high, a mile or so north of the town, so as to cut off the Turks from retreating up the Nablus road. We were, as Divisional Reserve, carrying full packs - not light fighting order - and it was an awful piece of country to cross without even a track. We had first to climb down some 600 feet into the Beit Iksa Wadi; then up the precipitous face of El Burj about 1000 feet from the bottom to the top; then a couple of comparatively easy miles down into the Wadi Hannina, and up the other side some 1200 feet to Tel-el-Ful. Our Battalion did not have to go very far beyond the Wadi Hannina, but we certainly thought it quite far enough. This was to be one of our worst nights, as it rained hard and blew a gale, and we were on the exposed side of the hill; also, no rations had arrived or were likely to arrive, nor was there any sign of them when we started off on a further advance north the next morning. However, we knew that Jerusalem had fallen, which cheered us up and made us hopeful that the operations would last less than the promised four days.

Our advance north was an attempt to get us into line with our own people on Neby Samwil, which was easily the most commanding feature of this part of the country. The battalion on our right had to attack up the exposed ridge along which ran the Nablus road, while we were lucky enough to have the frontage just east of the Wadi Hannina, where our objective, the steep and massive feature of Bab-el-Muallek covered us from artillery observation. The Turk soon spotted the movement and during our advance treated us to heavy shelling, which took a considerable toll from the exposed right battalion, whereas they were firing at us without observation, and did us no damage, though the machine-gunners, who advanced along with us, lost both men and mules. The actual crest of Bab-el-Muallek was most uncomfortable, as shells were bursting all along it; but though they searched the back of the hill most thoroughly, it was so steep that we were pretty safe so long as we lay snug. About 4 P.M. a couple of mules arrived with some rations. It did not go far, but was enough to give everyone a bite, and we were told that the rest would soon arrive.

Just on the top of this, we were told that the 60th Division was holding the line Tel-el-Ful-Beit Hannina, and that we might, as soon as we were ready, retire through them into support in the

Wadi Hannina. Not much time was lost in getting under way - we did not even wait for the Lewis gun mules, which were away being watered, but man-handled the guns and heavy valises. These proved really too heavy, and the men responsible for them were very much exhausted by the time we got into bivouac, though the distance cannot have been more than two or three miles. Here we found a regular haven of rest. Comparatively smooth, lying in an olive grove, and *all* the missing rations waiting for us. We ate about one whole day's rations in one enormous feed, and then went to sleep. We all needed it pretty badly, and even at dawn the whole camp was still sound asleep in spite of the fact that they had no covering but their greatcoats, and there was half an inch of ice on the water-buckets.

This proved to be the end of the Jerusalem push, and next day, 11th December, in glorious weather we marched back to a bivouac near Beit Iksa on the slopes of the wadi leading down from Neby Samwil to Kulonieh. Here we received our donkeys - forty per battalion - but they were in miserable condition and felt the cold terribly, most of them having come from the semi-tropical Nile Valley. They had also had a tough journey up, having had to carry loads most of the way from Railhead, when what they required was rest and food. Here we were within four miles of Jerusalem, and all ranks had the chance of seeing the city.

During the next week or so we managed to supplement our rations with dried figs, and the most excellent native brown bread; but the supply of the latter soon stopped, as we were forbidden to buy it, as it would just mean that the B.E.F. would have to supply bread to the population later on if we were allowed to consume their stocks of flour. H.Q. actually managed to secure a turkey, which was picketed out near the Quartermaster's stores to wait for Christmas. The programme here was "Road Improvement," but all the same we had a slack time for ten days or so, when we were told what was to be the next stunt. We were to assist in a big turning movement in which we were to go along the Zeitun Ridge, the object being the gaining of some elbow room to the north of Jerusalem. The 60th Division were to make an advance up the Nablus road, with which was to be combined a sweep by the 10th Division, with our Brigade attached, on to Bireh and Ram Allah from the west. The country favoured such a movement, as the main ridges ran east and west. We were to be at the same time the point of the echelon (the brigades being more or less echelonned from the right) and the inside of the wheel.

Our course lay along the Zeitun Ridge to Beitania, and on our left, and slightly in rear of us, brigades of the 10th Division were to sweep clear the Kereina Ridge south of the deep Wadi Ain Arik, and the Deir Ibzia-Ain Arik-Kefr Skeyan Ridges again farther to the north. This meant that we had to get back to our old home in the Wadi Zait, at the point where it joins the Wadi Selman, advance by night to the Wadi Imaish, which lay between Foka and Zeitun, and deploy there for the main attack. This was some twelve miles from Beit Iksa, and the preliminary reconnaissance was a hard day's work. We found that the 10th Division had, since we were there, secured Foka and Hill A, from which we got an excellent view of our objective - Zeitun - but we failed to find or hear of any path down to the Wadi Imaish. As nearly all the hills here about are steeply terraced, that meant we could take no mules with us to our position of deployment, as it would have been hopeless to have them clattering about on the rocks in the dark, and would have been certain to give the show away. We had expected to be able to do this assembly and approach in our own time, but through our secret service a copy was obtained of a Turkish order for an attack down the Nablus-Jerusalem road by two fresh divisions, timed for 6 A.M. on 27th December. This was only secured, however, three days in advance, and it was not till 3 P.M. on Christmas Eve that we got orders to move at once to our position of readiness in the Wadi Zait.

We hurriedly packed up, H.Q. cursing their luck at not being able to enjoy their turkey in peace, and got off about 6 P.M. Just after we started it began to rain heavily, and by 8 P.M., when the camel convoy tried to climb the hill out of the wadi, it was so slippery that they had to give it up. The quartermaster's hopes were then pinned on the donkeys, who were being tried for the first time, but the mud and cold proved too much for them. They managed to get most of them as far as Kubeibe - about half way - but they were quite incapable of going any farther. It was an awful night; such squalls and rain that the best mackintosh, much less greatcoat, was quite useless, and as our course lay along the Roman road we never left the exposed top of the ridge. It was not so bad while we were moving, but with a brigade in single file and a good many obstructions on the track, the rear of the column sometimes had to halt for half an hour while those in front negotiated some specially rough or slippery place.

Up till midnight there were fair intervals, and we kept on getting wet and then drying again; but midnight found us quite near our old camp at Q 20 central, fully exposed to a gale and torrents of rain.

The battalion in front of us had to descend the steep and slippery side of the Wadi Selman, which was just like a mud slide, and we had to stand at the top for more than half an hour. The length of the descent was only about 500 yards, and in the daylight and when it was dry fatigue parties and even camels used to get down in about ten minutes, but now, what with the rain and the passage of the unit in front of us, it had become indescribably slippery. Men were falling down every few yards, and the mules were not much better. It took two hours for the Battalion to cover this 500 yards.

Wishing each other a very happy Christmas, we started on the last stage of our journey along the bottom of the wadi, which was almost a river, to our pitch in the Wadi Zait. We sat there till dawn - sleep was out of the question - and then started everyone on physical drill to get up some circulation. By this time we knew that the camels and donkeys were both - in the language of the country - "mafisch" (which is the same as "nahpoo"), and also that the wheeled transport, which could not come across country as we had done, was not due till the afternoon. Even then it was unlikely that they would bring any food, as their proper load was Lewis gun stuff and ammunition. One can realise what disaster had overtaken even the best arrangements, when even Brigade H.Q., with a whole staff captain to look after them, hadn't so much as a crust for breakfast. The Brigadier, however, was as cheery as ever, and almost as soon as it was light he was up in our lines cracking jokes with everyone he met, and asking "are we downhearted," to which he got the usual roar as answer. It really never stopped raining all day, and never again it is to be hoped will any of us spend another Christmas like it. By superhuman efforts some few ration donkeys were persuaded along by their drivers, and arrived that night, but what they carried was only a small part of a ration. Our hopes were fixed on the wheeled transport, which had brought their loads of guns and ammunition, and had gone back to Kubeibe, to which half-way house our camel loads were being brought by the wheeled transport of the rest of the Division, who were not taking such a leading part in the coming stunt.

Next day, the 26th, was spent in reconnaissance by company officers who had not already done one, and in pow-wows at Brigade, at which were decided the final details and also the scheme under which the "B" teams were to undertake the carrying forward of ammunition and bombs in rear of the advance. Each battalion left behind some half dozen officers and about 50 men, so there was quite a fair number available for the work. Our spirits rose rapidly that day, partly owing to the prospect of something doing, partly because of a marked improvement in the weather, but chiefly on account of the arrival of rations in satisfying quantities, which allowed of a huge feed before we had to start at about 10.30 P.M. There was a nice moon, and our march in single file up the Wadi Zait to Foka was quite uneventful, and we got a pleasant surprise when we topped the crest and found that, by pure luck, we had struck a small footpath - the only one for miles, we afterwards discovered - which made the descent beautifully easy and comparatively silent. With some diffidence we made for what we thought was our map reference, and found to our joy, that we were exactly right. Our "perch," as really it should be called, was on numerous ledges on the face of a very steep cliff, and it was a lengthy business getting the Battalion arranged with its different companies respectively in their right places; but by 4 A.M. we were all snug like gannets on the Bass Rock, and quite easy in our minds, except for the uncertainty as to whether dawn would discover the place to be under Turkish machine-gun fire. This was pretty important, as we were not to attack until 8 A.M., so there was time for a very uncomfortable two or three hours before we could start. However, dawn broke, and all was quiet, and we were able to have our breakfast undisturbed just about the time the Turks must have been attacking down the Nablus-Jerusalem road.

The first attack was to be led by the Ayr and Lanarks on the right, who were to scale the salient spur running up to their objective - Kh. Mahmeh, and by the Somersets on the left, who were to advance up the spur which led in a N.E. direction to Sh. Abu-el-Zeitun, which was their objective. We, in close support, and the Devons in reserve, were to follow the left battalion. This plan was adopted to avoid having to advance up the re-entrant which was too dangerous.

At 8 A.M. the advance started. Our position was in close support, and the chief difficulty was to prevent the leading lines from going too fast, and getting mixed up with the battalion in front. By 9 A.M. the ridge was taken with a nice little bunch of prisoners, and very few casualties to us. The face, up which we had advanced, was so steep that the defenders could not get a really good shot at us, except in certain places; but the Somersets and ourselves had to slide to the east side of the spur, as we were being heavily fired at by machine guns from the direction of Kh. Kereina.

Our programme now was to turn east and sweep along the Zeitun Ridge, but this depended, to some extent, on how the 10th Division were getting on to our left. We were intended to be in advance of them, but not more than a mile or so or we should get it too badly from the flank. They had not expected us to get Zeitun much before 11 A.M., so we were ahead of time, and the brigade on our left must have been a bit late, as it was some time before they were visible at all, and then they were some three miles behind. We sat all day on the safer side of the crest, watching a stubbornly contested battle being fought on Hill 2450, which was taken and lost more than once, and in getting shelled continually by field guns. They did not hit many, but, as bad luck would have it, they got our adjutant, Captain W.D. Brown, as game a fellow as ever walked, and he was carried off evidently very badly hit, and died that night in the dressing-station. We were not at the time in touch with Brigade, but the brigade-major was over on the ridge with us, so we had to get out orders for the further advance.

It was our Battalion's turn to lead, and we went for the main objective, the Hill of Shafa, at the extreme end of the ridge about one and a half miles away. The Ayrs and Lanarks were sent to seize a hill on our right, another to maintain touch with the 10th Division on our left (we were responsible as far as the W. Sunt), and the fourth in support of us. We started the advance just after dark, and all went well until we had almost reached the objective. One could see the other battalion in the moonlight on the crest of the lesser hill to our right, and we were ourselves about half way up Shafa, when we suddenly bumped right into the Turk. Both sides were rather taken by surprise, and our men at all events were thoroughly excited and firing wildly in the dark without much chance of hitting anything. There was a natural rock face about 8 feet deep right across the face of the hill, and only about two spots where it could be climbed, and this held us up for some time. The Turk began to try to work round the flanks and the situation was looking rather unpleasant, especially as we were wasting, at a great rate, ammunition which might be badly wanted next day, the Lewis guns expending thousands.

However, shortly before midnight, the excitement calmed down a bit, and we managed to get up the rock face on to a sort of false crest, and scouts, sent out to the front, reported that the Turk had cleared right off the whole hill. Two platoons advanced and occupied the farther crest and then we settled down to get what rest we could though it was too cold to sleep, and a good many spent most of the night walking up and down to keep warm. We found next day that our ammunition had not been entirely wasted, as there were a lot of dead Turks and quantities of rifles and machine-gun equipment left behind when they retreated. Our casualties that night were 2 officers and 7 other ranks killed, and 22 other ranks wounded, 3 of whom died of wounds.

In the morning we expected orders to advance, but as soon as we could use our glasses we found that we were far ahead of our neighbours, and were, in fact, enfiladed from the Turkish positions on our left. Fortunately we could get into cover by going about 100 yards round the hill, but rations and supplies had to come across about 80 yards of open, under machine-gun fire, and it was a marvel that no one was hit. It was impossible to get out in front to see our next objective, as the Turks had us well marked and machine guns opened on anyone who exposed himself. We had the Brigade-Major with us, but were again out of touch with Brigade, and Lieut.-Colonel Younger was again tackling the dispositions for the next advance, when the Brigadier himself rode up, very nearly getting sniped as he trotted in. After telling us exactly what he thought of us for having chosen such an exposed place for our headquarters, he got out his orders for the assault of Beitania. There was really no choice as to who should go first this time, as there was no time to reshuffle units, and they just had to go over in the order in which they were at the time disposed.

This made us right leading battalion - objective Beitania - with the Ayrs and Lanarks in close support. The left leading battalion - the Somersets - were to make for Hill 500 about three-quarters of a mile north of Beitania. The Devons were to advance in close support of the Somersets, and we were given the K.S.L.I. from the 231st Brigade to remain in reserve on Shafa, where Brigade H.Q. also remained. The left battalion also had El Muntar as a further objective, so that the Brigade, when finished, would be on a line running north and south to the Wadi Kelt. We knew we should get a warm reception going over the crest, as there were quite a number of machine guns in the village and they were all laid on the crest. They also put over a lot of shells while we were preparing to start but did not do much damage.

We got off the mark at 2 P.M. in four waves, and went at record speed to the bottom of the ravine. One could hardly have believed that men carrying Lewis guns could have covered the ground so fast. In this case it was our salvation, as we not only got over before the whole of the machine guns had got properly going, but most of the shelling also fell behind us. Once in the bottom we were quite safe from the machine guns, and nearly so from the artillery. As it was we reorganised for the attack in our own time and were very soon at the edge of the village after a precipitous climb. Here we were held up for a short time by fire from a spur to our right. The leading Company Commander, Captain P. Campbell, A. & L.Y., of the supporting battalion, agreed to take his own and another company to clear this spur. This movement was rapidly and brilliantly carried out with the desired result, and in a very short time we were in the village and through the far side, holding the ridge to left and right, and in touch with our left battalion. It was not until the following morning that we began to count the spoils, which ran to about 150 prisoners, including a battalion commander and nine machine guns. We buried about 80 Turks, and there were a good many in odd places that we didn't find at the time. That night we took up an outpost line east of the village, and in the morning saw the 230th Brigade march across our front into Bireh without firing a shot. So well, too, had the supply of ammunition worked, that at the close of operations we had 50,000 rounds in Beitania. We spent two days there clearing up the battlefield and reorganising the companies. On the second night we were told that we were to be taken out into reserve for a long and well-earned rest.

From St James's Park to Beitania the Battalion had been continuously engaged in very strenuous operations, marching, fighting, or road-making over the roughest of country, without roads or landmarks, up precipitous hills, through boulder-strewn wadis, against an obstinate and determined foe, never sure of the next meal, tired almost beyond endurance and many almost bootless, in the worst of weather, cold and wet, and only slightly less miserable than the camels. And the result? The capture of Jerusalem and turning of the Turkish left flank; a loss of prestige and a military disaster from which they never recovered. We had taken part in most difficult and arduous fighting in most difficult and arduous country; difficult because of the badness of the maps, which made it almost impossible to locate one's position or maintain touch, and arduous as only those who know that rocky precipitous country can realise. For artillery it was practically impossible, and though they did wonders in bringing guns up over the roughest of roadless hills, the assistance they could render the infantry was very slight. Nor are the transport or camel leaders likely to forget that trek, and it was greatly to Mr Drysdale's credit that he managed to get them all safely to Kubeibeh early on the morning of the 8th December. The heavy rains made the

Roman road almost impossible, and troops "resting" (so-called) were turned on to road-making. The difficulty of command may be illustrated by the fact that in marching to Beit Iksa the whole Battalion was strung out in single file along a sheep track.

It was very largely owing to this threat on his line of retirement that caused the evacuation of Jerusalem which was entered by our troops on 9th December. On the 8th 1 officer and 50 other ranks had gone to Enab to furnish guards for Jerusalem, and to this Battalion fell the honour of supplying the first Christian guards over the holy places in Jerusalem after a Moslem occupation of seven centuries.

Beitania, which brought the operations to a close, was quite a brilliant piece of work. Our casualties were 1 officer and 8 other ranks killed, and 4 officers and 40 other ranks wounded, of whom 2 subsequently died of wounds; but, as we found afterwards that Zeitun and Beitania had both been held by picked fresh troops, whose morale had not been tried by the continuous fighting of the November retreat, that number could not be called excessive.

To single out individuals when everyone did so well is an invidious task, but one cannot close an account of these operations without mentioning the really splendid work of Lieut.-Colonel Younger, Captain H.S. Sharp, and Captain W.D. Brown, also of Lieutenant R.A. Andrew, whose energy and determination in bringing up rations and ammunition over the most Godforsaken country, cannot be too highly praised.

The news of the previous night proved to be correct, and the Battalion moved off from Beitania about 9 A.M. on New Year's Day down the Wadi Sunt. The Wadi Sunt was by far the most attractive wadi we had yet struck, being steep sided, and on the south side especially clothed not only with the usual olive tree, but also with many sorts of creepers and wild flowers which we had not seen before. The whole side rose in terraces, and from almost every terrace, overhanging on to the one below, was a very pretty dark leaved creeper, which was at the time in full bloom with clusters of creamy coloured flowers which looked as if they were made of wax, and the ledges were carpeted with various wild flowers, mostly cyclamen and anemone. A mile or two took us to the junction of the Wadis Sunt and Imaish, where we were within a few hundred yards of the ledges where we had perched before taking Zeitun Ridge, and there it began to rain in torrents. We continued down the Sunt until we came to a rough path, made more or less possible for traffic by the 10th Division, which led up to Beit-ur-el-Tahta, in the neighbourhood of which the Brigade was to bivouac. Next day we proceeded via the Wadi Melab to Beit Sira, and so to our rest camp at Yalo.

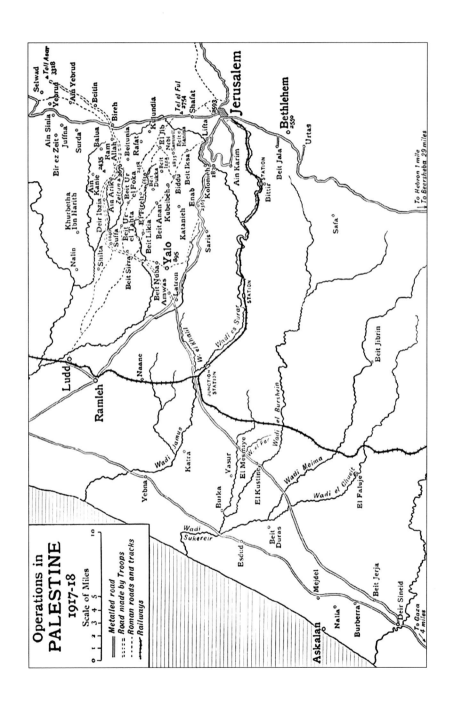

Operations in
PALESTINE
1917-18
Scale of Miles

_____ Metalled road
:::::::: Road made by Troops
- - - - Roman roads and tracks
╫╫╫╫ Railways

Selwad
Tell Asur 3318
Ain Sinia
Bir ez Zeit
Juffna
Yebrud
Ain Yebrud
Surda
Beitin
Balua
Ram Allah
Bireh
Khurbetha Ibn Harith
Deir Ibzia
Ain Kanie
2435
Suffa
Zeitun
Kilundia
Tel el Ful 2754
Shafat
Beit Unia
Rafat
Jerusalem 2593
Beitunia
Nalin
Shilta
Ain Arik
Beit Ur el Foka
El Tire
Beituma
El Jib
Nebi Samwil
Beit Iksa
Rafat
Bethlehem 2550
Urtas
Beit Ur el Tahta
Beit Sirra
Beit Likia
Beit Anan
Beit Duka
Biddu
Hanina
Lifta
Beit Jala
To Hebron 1 mile
To Beersheba 29 miles
Beit Nuba
Kubeibeh
Katanieh
Enab
Kolonieh 1830
Ain Karim
Bittir
Amwas
Yalo 905
Katanieh
Saris
STATION
Safa
Latron
Beit Jibrin
Naane
W. el Khalil
Wadi es Surat
STATION
Ludd
Ramleh
JUNCTION STATION
Wadi el Burshein
Katra
Wadi Jamus
Yasur
Wadi el Far
Wadi Meima
Yebna
Burka
El Mesmiye
El Kustine
Wadi el Ghuett
El Faluje
Esdud
Wadi Sukereir
Beit Duras
Mejdel
Beit Jerja
Askalan
Nalia
Burberra
Deir Sineid
To Gaza 4 miles

- CHAPTER V -
PALESTINE - 1918

FROM 4TH JANUARY TO 14th March when we went into the line at Khan Abu Felah, we were employed continuously on road-making. The great difficulty experienced in bringing supplies forward over the roadless mountainous country, impassable to motors and often even to camels and mules, made road-making an absolute necessity before any further advance could take place. The only metalled roads were the Jerusalem-Nablus road, running north from Jerusalem, and the Jerusalem-Jaffa road, running west and north-west, passing Latron about four miles from our camp at Yalo. The rest were mere donkey tracks over cultivated unbottomed ground in the valleys, and winding up wadis, over boulders, and through trees in the uplands and hills.

Yalo, the ancient Ajalon, a city of the tribe of Dan, was our camp till 24th February. Brigade H.Q. were at the head of the next wadi to us, and below them the Devons and Somersets, while we occupied the other side of the ridge with the 229th Field Ambulance beyond us. The Ayrs and Lanarks were in a separate camp at Amwas. When we arrived we found a rocky barren hill - when we left, it was almost a garden city. The only "houses" were Battalion H.Q. and the kitchens, but every two or three had built a home for themselves out of stones and mud, roofed with waterproof sheets, while JOCK'S LODGE, a company sergeants' mess, was quite an architectural triumph. Paths lined with stones ran in all directions, and almost every "villa" had its little garden of wild flowers, chiefly scarlet anemones transplanted from the wadi. Below us was the Valley of Ajalon, where Joshua defeated the kings of the Amorites and the moon was stayed, a rich fertile plain stretching to the hills which circled it on three sides. North-east we could see nestling in the hills the two Beth Horons, and south of us lay the picturesque capital of the tribe of Dan.

While we were still settling down we sent 4 officers and 200 other ranks daily on road-making fatigue, but later on the entire battalion was turned on to repair the road from Latron to Beit Sara. At the same time Captain Andrew was busy with a large class teaching the Lewis gun to officers and men, Mr Scott's flags "spoke" from every knoll, and Mr Gall smartened the backward squad on the drill-ground below. We had quite a good rifle range, and quite a fair football field, and life was really very pleasant.

On 18th February Lieut.-Colonel Younger rejoined us. He had gone off to Cairo on leave where he was seized by Dr Tuke and put to bed in the Citadel.

We had now pretty well completed our road, so on the 24th we left our comfortable camp and marched six miles to our new bivouac area in an olive grove just north of Beit Sira. We had to make a new road to link up with the Ram Allah road at Tattenham Corner. It was a most picturesque wadi covered with olive trees, and what was more important with any amount of stones suitable for road-making just at hand. On the Latron-Beit Sira road stones were scarce and had to be man-handled in limbers or baskets often quite a distance, but here were stones of every size within a few yards of the road. It was a 16-foot road bottomed with large stones, then two layers of smaller stones and blinded with gravel. Everyone went at it like a schoolboy on holiday, and we completed our road two days before scheduled time, on one occasion actually doing 1½ yards of road per man.

On 5th March we left our camp going by our newly completed road to Tattenham Corner, into the Wadi Ain Arik, and up the Wadi Sad to our halting place not far from the village of Ain Arik. We were now campaigning again and our baggage was cut down to the bare establishment, with one notable exception - oatmeal. We had arranged for a regular supply from home to start as soon as we went abroad, and though we were often short of many things we always had our oatmeal. Our supplies had accumulated while we had been in the hills, and we now found ourselves with about 30 cwt. for which there was no room on the transport. This we were absolutely determined not to lose, so we sent it on ahead about ten miles and dumped it in a wadi with a couple of men to look after it.

Next day we continued our journey through Ain Arik, where a friendly brass band played us past with "Bonnie Dundee" till just below the top of the pass at Kefr Skeyan, where we rested for the afternoon as we might not cross the skyline in daylight. This resulted in a most tedious night march, finishing in pitch darkness over very rough going with a bad bivouac area at the end of it. Next morning we were surprised to find ourselves by the side of a small lake - Lake Baluah - shallow and muddy, but welcome as giving water for the animals quite close to their lines. Road-making near Ram Allah was the order of the day, and one company anyhow found the return journey not without its excitement. A Taube dived at them and opened fire at very close range, but fortunately their aim was distinctly bad, and it was our nervous system only that suffered.

We were now only a few miles behind the line, and though our Brigade was only to be in support for the next advance the C.O. and Company Commanders climbed Sheikh Abdullah, from which a good view of the surrounding country could be obtained. This was an easy climb, but the view from here showed us that the next advance would be no picnic even if the country alone had to be overcome. Ridge upon ridge faced us, rising higher and higher to the horizon about six miles away where Burj Lisaneh stood up like a sugar-loaf, while to our half-right steepish slopes covered with fig trees, not yet in leaf, rose up to the heights of Tel

BATTALION BIVOUAC, NEAR SUFFA.

THE IRISH ROAD CROSSING THE WADI AIN ARIK.

Asur 3318 feet high. In all this country there was but one road which wound its way among the hills towards Nablus (the ancient Shechem) and the north. There were a few miles of road up as far as Beitin (the Bethel of the Bible), but there it stopped short, which meant that the 53rd Division on our right would have to do their advance without any road at all; but we had all done without roads before, and no doubt we should do equally well again. However, we had now completed a road through from Latron to Ram Allah and the Nablus road, so that a further advance was possible as supplies could now be brought up. The corps had been more or less stationary across the Jerusalem-Nablus road for six or seven weeks, though there had been a lot of activity on the eastern flank towards Jericho.

On 8th March B Company (Captain D.D. Ogilvie) started off to report to the gunners near Ain Yebrud and make the track passable for the artillery as far as Selwad on the far side of Tel Asur. The track was a dry river bed between two very thick walls most of the way, and where it was impassable a track had to be made across country, which meant cutting down trees and levelling terraces. Though there was about five miles of road to prepare, so well did they work at it that they were actually working on the road in front of the supports before Tel Asur was finally captured, and the guns were able to move forward that night.

Meanwhile the other three companies had gone up the Nablus road to repair it, as it had not only been heavily shelled by our artillery but also blown up in a great many places by the retreating Turks. The enemy were offering a stout resistance to our advance, and held a strong line across the road. Tel Asur was captured and lost three times before it finally remained in our hands, and it was not until 1 P.M. that our line was sufficiently far forward for us to proceed to Ain Sinia for road repair. Even then the road was being so heavily shelled that we had to make our way by side paths and across country. We were busy road-repairing for the next day or two, and officers were reconnoitring forward to see the lie of the country which we were to take over.

On 14th March we moved on again, halting behind the skyline for the midday meal while the C.O. and Company Commanders went on to see the line we were to take over. It had been a rough journey. The tracks were positively heart breaking. The usual pattern was 4 to 6 feet wide with stout drystone walls on either side; the "pathway" being over rough and uneven rocks with an occasional boulder, and here and there the walls had collapsed completely, blocking the track - or else over cultivated soil which was immediately converted into a muddy morass of uncertain depth. On such paths only single file was possible, and pack mules and donkeys had to be almost carried over some of the places. But the worst was yet to come, and though we were not intended to go down into the Wadi Kolah by day as it was in full view to the Turkish artillery, the track down was so bad the C.O. wisely preferred risking a shell or two to certain suicide going down in the dark. A mist helped us, and we got down unmolested and had taken over the new line by 5 P.M. The track down into the wadi was so steep and slippery from the rain that donkeys were actually lowered down in some places by their tails.

The line we took over was a long one - about two and a half miles - previously held by nine companies of the 159th and 160th Brigades (53rd Division). There were three mountains with steep wadis in between, and each company was given a hill which formed an isolated post. Touch even between companies was very difficult to maintain at night, and touch with the units on either flank was found impossible and had to be abandoned. So sketchy was our line that we sometimes discovered in the morning a miserable Turk or Arab well inside our lines trying to desert but finding no one to whom to surrender. When "captured" their joy was complete. Miserable, half-starved, ill-clad wretches, conscripted to fight for a nation they loathed and feared.

D Company (Captain J. M'Nab) held the Round Hill on the right and a platoon of A Company held the village of Khan Abu Felah. C Company (Captain I.C. Nairn) held the centre hill and B Company (Captain D.D. Ogilvie) were on the left holding a "hog's back" known as Fusilier Ridge, and the wadi on either side. A Company (Captain Sir W.A.A. Campbell) were in reserve at Battalion H.Q. Later A Company relieved D Company, and D and C Companies moved a hill to their left, while B came into reserve. Our horses, mules, and donkeys were with us, but camels could not negotiate the steep slopes and remained on the high ground above us along with the wheeled transport.

Our stay here was uneventful. The Turks shelled us regularly but without doing much damage, and we sent over one or two patrols every night, but there was no great activity on either side. On 22nd March a company of the Ayrs and Lanarks (Captain P. Campbell) carried out a most successful raid on the isolated hill Amurieh opposite B Company. Mr Cruickshank with 12 men from his platoon held White Hill, a small intermediate knoll, and covered the advance, returning when the raid started. Fully 100 prisoners were taken, with the loss of only one or two wounded. At the same time we made a demonstration from Kent Hill, firing off rifle grenades and rifles, which drew a lot of fire from the raiding party on Amurieh.

On 7th April the enemy attempted a bombing raid on A Company's hill, but it was a halfhearted affair, and they were easily driven off and a few casualties inflicted.

We had two or three days of very heavy rain just after we took over, which made life very miserable for the outpost companies on the hill tops, and especially for the mule leaders who had to make the journey up and down that perilous wadi with rations and water at least once and sometimes twice a day, and then wade through the mud to the companies. The rain, however, helped them, as it gave us water close at hand which was excellent for cooking and washing purposes. On the whole, however, the weather was glorious, and the wild flowers were a great joy to us all.

After we had done a fortnight in the line we were to have been relieved by another battalion in the Brigade when news came through that the whole Division was to be relieved and march to Railhead, which was now at Ludd. This, combined with a memo, which said "All units XX. Corps except 74th Division will indent for shorts forthwith," made it quite clear that we were bound for France, and so it proved.

On 9th April we were relieved by the 2/4 R.W.F. (53rd Division), and bivouacked that night at our transport lines on the shoulder of Tel Asur. Next day the Brigade marched via Beitin to Bireh and bivouacked just west of Ram Allah. The following day we went down the Ain Arik road to Tattenham Corner, along the road we ourselves had made to our bivouac area, near the old Devon Camp below Suffa.

On 12th April we made Amwas, and next day after a long and dusty march we reached our destination Ludd. We spent a busy day there drawing stores from Ordnance and returning things for which we had no further use. H.Q. and B Company entrained that evening, and the remainder the following morning, and we all got to Kantara that night, or very early on the morning of the 16th.

We were at Kantara just a fortnight, during which time we were disinfected and refitted, put through gas and exercised in field days on the desert. We had never been allowed to draw clothing in Palestine after Yalo as we were on the waiting list for France, and when we arrived at Kantara we were a most disreputable looking crowd - clothing patched and torn, garments showing where they should never be seen, and boots in some cases almost without soles at all. But when we marched out we were clad once more in new tunics, new trousers, and new boots, and looked very smart.

The transport left on 19th April under Mr J. Drysdale, and the Battalion followed on the 29th, reaching Alexandria early next morning, and embarking at once on H.M.T. *Indarra*. Brigade H.Q. were with us. Lieut.-Colonel Younger was O.C. troops, and Mr R. Colthart, ship's adjutant.

We left Alexandria on 1st May, and so bade good-bye to Egypt and the East after a sojourn there of over two and a half years. We had all had a great experience, at times very strenuous and unpleasant, but on the whole interesting and not too bad. Our fighting had been almost entirely open warfare, for which as yeomanry we were well adapted, and which contrasted very favourably with the trench warfare on the Western Front. But few were sorry to go. None of us anticipated Allenby's triumphant drive to Damascus, and felt we would be "doing our bit" more effectively on the Western Front where we well knew the final decision rested. But what counted much more was relief at escaping another hot, dusty, thirsty summer in the East, and the change to the civilisation and comparative comfort of France, and of course most of all to the proximity of Blighty, and the prospect of leave home. Though short local leave had not been so difficult to obtain, home leave, owing to the difficulty of transportation, had been very much restricted, and the great majority had never been home since coming out.

We had a very good trip to Marseilles. The captain laid himself out to make everything as comfortable as possible; the feeding was excellent, plenty of cabin accommodation for officers and N.C.O.'s, and the men were as comfortable as they ever can be in a crowded troopship. There were seven ships in the convoy which was escorted by British destroyers as far as Malta, and there relieved by Japanese destroyers who took us in safely to Marseilles. There was only one piece of excitement on the fourth day out. A destroyer sighted a submarine, rushed ahead at great speed and dropped a couple of depth charges. Nothing more was seen of the submarine, and we proceeded on our journey uninterrupted.

- CHAPTER VI -
FRANCE - 1918

ON DISEMBARKING AT MARSEILLES on 7th May we opened a new chapter in the history of the Regiment. The contrast from the East was indeed marked and delightful, and the long train journey passed quickly in our joy at seeing once more green fields and green trees, villages, and farms, long fair hair and fair complexions. We could hardly have had more beautiful scenery than we had during the first day through the south of France. We kept to the branch lines to the west of the main Rhone Valley line, and wound in and out all day at the foot of steep hills crowned with old castles and picturesque villages which looked so peaceful that it was hard to realise that there was a war on. The second day saw us skirting Paris by Juvisy, and gave us a good view of Versailles and the numerous airships at St Cyr. The last day our route lay chiefly through water meadows, and by 9.30 we had reached our detraining station - Noyelles - whence after a hot breakfast we marched ten miles to our destination - St Firmin near the mouth of the Somme. Our transport had already been here about a week, and we found excellent quarters in the long straggling village.

Here we spent ten days, being fitted out with gas helmets, and passed through gas, a form of warfare of which we had had no practical experience out East, and in bayonet fighting also, under experts who found we had not very much to learn in that line. Our number of Lewis guns were doubled, and we started lots of classes of new Lewis gunners to form the new gun crews and provide a large nucleus of trained men as reinforcements. Our transport establishment was also completed here. We entrained at Rue early on the morning of the 21st, and made our way via Etaples and St Pol to Ligny St Flochel, whence we had a long fifteen miles march to Humbercourt. That night we had our first experience of night bombing. From here several senior officers went for a day or two's experience of trench life to a New Zealand Division in the Hebuterne sector north of Albert.

On the 25th May we moved to a very much better area at Grand Rullecourt where we stayed for just a month. Here there were much better facilities for training, and we worked away steadily at wood fighting, fighting through crops, co-operation with tanks, and all the while paying special attention to the Lewis-gun personnel. We also gave an exhibition of the attack in open warfare, for the edification of the Canadians who were in the neighbourhood, and put in a good deal of musketry at the rifle ranges, and throwing and firing grenades. We had quite a good field for football, and had an inter-platoon competition, won by No. 6 platoon, but the great event was the defeat of the Scots Guards by the Battalion team. The Scots Guards were the winners of the Bull Dog Cup at the Crystal Palace, and had only once been beaten, and to defeat them 2-0 was a great achievement.

The Ayr and Lanark Battalion of the R.S.F. left us here to form a new brigade along with the 12th (Norfolk Yeomanry) Battalion; the Norfolk Regiment from the 230th Brigade, and the 24th (Denbigh Yeomanry) Battalion; the Royal Welsh Fusiliers from the 231st Brigade. We were all very depressed at the departure of the Ayrs and Lanarks. We had been together close friends and keen rivals on the football field ever since we had been made into an infantry battalion, and though we all knew that the Brigade was sure to be reduced from four to the normal French establishment of three battalions, we had somehow never contemplated parting from our special friends, the only other Scotch battalion in the Division.

Spanish influenza, which was so prevalent everywhere, now began to attack us, and when we left Grand Rullecourt on 26th

June, as we had about nine miles to march to our entraining station Ligny, 150 were considered unfit to march, and had to come on by motor lorry the following day. This was an excellent arrangement, as it enabled us to keep on the men who we knew would be quite fit again in a day or two, instead of sending them to hospital, and probably to another battalion. Fortunately it was a mild type, the patient being completely knocked out for a day or two and then rapidly recovering, but it left us all pretty weak for a bit. We detrained at Aire, and though we had only another four miles to go to our billets at Fontes, it was quite enough for anyone with a touch of the "'flu." From here parties went out every day to reconnoitre the various lines in the Robecq-St Venant sector, and to get to know the country before we were told to take over the line.

We left Fontes with practically all our invalids cured after a fortnight's stay, and moved on to Ham en Artois, only a few miles farther east, where we became Divisional Reserve, our Division having taken over a sector of the line in the Lys area. Here we carried on our company and specialist training while parties reconnoitred forward, and after twelve days in reserve we again made a short move forward on 23rd July to La Pierriere where we became Brigade Reserve, the Brigade having the other two battalions now in the line. This was a strenuous business, as not only had we to provide small working parties by day and guards over about eleven bridges over the Aire-La Bassée Canal, but we had also to supply 100 men per company each night to dig in the support line, which meant very hard work for both company officers and men, and it was with relief that we saw our eight days finished, and moved ourselves into the line. It was not that the digging was such hard or jumpy work, but the fact that it took two hours to get there and two more to come back, which made it such a trying business. There were very few casualties, though B Company had a lucky escape. A shell landed right in the middle of them and wounded thirteen, five of whom had to go to hospital, while the other eight asked to remain on duty, fearing lest, if they went to hospital, they might be posted to another battalion.

On the night of 31st July/1st August, we took over the right sub-sector of the line from the Somersets, and were lucky in having to keep only one company in the line. This front line consisted of a series of posts, each held by a section and built up as a breastwork, trenches being impossible. The Noc and Clarence Rivers sluggishly meandered through our line, and even in summer the water level was only about nine inches below the surface. Behind these posts was a semi-continuous support line, and half a mile farther back a continuous main line, fairly well complete as to wire and parapet, but hardly anything in the way of parados, so there was plenty of work for everyone. D Company (Captain R.A. Andrew) held the front line with their H.Q. at Baquerolles Farm, A and B Companies were in support, and C back at Robecq in reserve. Battalion H.Q. were at Carvin Farm. Frequent patrols were sent out, and the Bosche paid us a certain amount of attention both with high explosives and gas, and at night turned on his machine guns along the routes by which rations came up, but at no time could it have been called anything but a quiet sector.

We had been six days in the line when about four o'clock in the afternoon word came from the battalion on the left that the enemy were massing in front. Captain Andrew at once sent out officers' patrols who discovered no signs of the enemy, so he took his company forward and occupied the German trenches, and by evening held a line about half a mile farther forward. It was now evident that the enemy intended evacuating the salient which our gunners had made so unpleasant for him for some time past, and by nightfall our whole line was moving forward. To D Company fell the distinction of initiating the advance on the whole corps' front, and then B Company passed through them and advanced the line to Rues des Vaches Farm. So rapid had been our advance that a party of Germans, still under the impression that they were behind their own lines, bumped right into a section of Mr Wood's platoon in a "grouse butt." On being challenged, the Bosche sergeant-major called out, "Welche Kompanie ist das?" (which company is that?) which seemed to annoy one Jock who replied "Welsh Company be damned. Take that, you —, it's the Black Watch you're up against this time." Their carelessness cost them five killed, including the sergeant-major, and twice as many wounded.

Next day we advanced to just beyond the Quentin Road, meeting with practically no opposition, and later A Company (Mr C.G. Duncan) passed through B, and advanced to the Turbeauté River. The Bosche guns were very busy all day, and considering the number of shells they threw over us and our lack of any cover, we were lucky in having as few casualties as we did. We had a good deal of gas in our area and on the main road, and the following day after a short but severe trench-mortar bombardment they attacked one of our posts on the Turbeauté River which repulsed them at the point of the bayonet. That night we were relieved by the 15th Battalion, the Suffolk Regiment (230th Brigade); our relief was managed quite successfully, and we went back into support at Robecq, with garrisons in the main line of the Amusoires trench system.

Only very short parade hours and daily bathes in the Lys or La Bassée Canals made this a delightful week. We were asked for no digging parties, and the only fatigue - which the men thoroughly enjoyed - was harvesting under Mr H. Adamson's supervision.

On 16th August we moved a few miles farther back across the Canal to La Miquellerie where we had as good billets as we had seen in France. Up to now we had received a few kilts of the large size only, so we had only a few of the biggest men fitted out, and drill order was always trousers. On getting to Miquellerie we found a huge assortment of kilts awaiting us, and the sergeant-tailor (Sergeant Ferguson) had two hectic days fitting the Battalion for the Divisional Church Parade in a field between La

Miquellerie and Ham en Artois. The Army Commander, General Sir Wm. Birdwood, was present, and after the service he gave us a most inspiring address, and saw us march past him in fours as we left the field. The two following days were devoted to a detailed inspection by the Corps Commander, Lieut.-General Sir R. Haking, who seemed favourably impressed and made some very complimentary remarks.

On the 24th we moved up into support relieving the 25th R.W.F. The Battalion was disposed in two halves supporting the right and left battalions respectively - A and C Companies at Quentin and B and D Companies in front of Calonne with Battalion H.Q. After spending three quiet days here we were relieved by the 2/6th Battalion D.L.I. (59th Division), and marched back to Molinghem where our transport had been all the time. B Company left that afternoon, and the rest of the Battalion entrained next day on a tactical train for the Somme. We had a very slow journey, and arrived at La Houssoye about midnight and found our billets there. On 31st August the B Team moved to the Divisional Reception Camp at Franvillers, and about midday we got sudden orders to proceed to near Franvillers where buses would be awaiting us. We went by bus to a farm a couple of miles west of Maricourt, dumped our packs there and reached our destination Le Foret about midnight, where to our joy we were run to earth by the transport with rations and ammunition.

Next day, 1st September, was spent in reconnaissance towards Bouchavesnes, out of which the Bosche had been pushed that morning. At 7.30 P.M. we set out for the position of deployment east of Bouchavesnes, and were met by guides who conducted us by the longest possible route over the worst country they could find, and it was 3 A.M. before the relief of the 2/4th London Regiment was complete and our men in the assembly trenches. Zero hour was 5.30 A.M., at which time it was barely light and rather misty. The first objective was the system of trenches (Opera and Monastir Trenches) on the far side of the Canal Du Nord, the second objective the strong system of trenches half way up the slope, and the final objective the crest of the ridge south of Nurlu Village, a good four miles away. We were to advance across the Tortille River keeping Moislains on our left, across the Canal and then swing northeast and push on to the high ground. This meant squeezing through a narrow neck between Moislains and Allaines and then after we were through the neck, changing direction and extending our front to almost double.

After the preliminary bombardment and following the creeping barrage the Brigade moved forward - the Somersets leading on the right with ourselves following. The Devons were to mop up the village of Moislains, and once clear of the village we were to come up on the left of the Somersets and take the first objective. The barrage fell a long way ahead of us and left untouched a party of the enemy holding the trench immediately in front of us. This delayed us but for a moment, but the Somersets were having a good deal of trouble from the direction of Allaines which had to be dealt with and this took them and us more to our right than we should have been. The advance was again momentarily held up by heavy machine-gun fire on the Canal, but pushing on in most gallant style the leading companies got across all right and up the slope, driving the Bosche out of the wooden huts at the point of the bayonet and accounting for a great many at the same time. So far the advance had gone splendidly. The first objective had been taken, and the advance begun towards the second when murderous machine-gun fire was opened upon us from the left and left rear. The battalion of Londoners on our left north of Moislains had withdrawn, the village of Moislains itself was never mopped up, and the eight Bosche machine-guns holding Moislains seeing this moved quickly to the south of the village and opened on our backs. In addition to this we were being subjected to very heavy fire on our left flank, which was now completely in the air, and we could actually see their gun teams working the 77's on the crest of the ridge. The Bosche had paid us the compliment of rushing up his best troops to meet our Division, and certainly the Alpini Corps were most gallant fighters. To advance unsupported was out of the question, and our casualties were by now very heavy, so there was nothing left but to withdraw to the west side of the Canal again and reorganise the remains of the companies. Next day we pushed forward to the trenches south of Moislains and to the Slag Heap on the canal bank, and at dusk on the evening of the 4th we were relieved by the 19th Battalion London Regiment and marched back to rest and reorganise.

Our casualties had been heavy - the C.O. wounded; of the four Company Commanders Captain R.W. Stewart and Captain I.C. Nairn had been killed and Captain J. M'Nab and Mr C.G. Duncan wounded. Mr Darney was killed and C.S.M. Aitken died of wounds - a total of 3 officers and 38 other ranks killed and 14 officers and 157 other ranks wounded. The Battalion got great praise for its gallant performance that day, and though the attack was apparently unsuccessful we had advanced farther than the authorities had expected, and, moreover, had the pleasure of seeing the 230th Brigade, who passed through us, make good about six miles without firing a shot - a peace march, which as Brig.-General Hoare was at pains to point out was entirely due to the offensive spirit of the 229th Brigade.

We were given a day and a half in which to rest and reorganise and then off again on the retreating Bosche. Just as we were leaving we heard that Mr J.C. Drysdale had been hit by a shell which landed right at the mouth of his bivouac, at least six miles behind the line. In him we lost a most efficient and hard-working transport officer. After a night at Aizecourt and another at Longavesnes we were again in the line relieving the 25th (Montgomery and Welsh Horse Yeomanry) Battalion Welsh Regiment in the left sector of the divisional front holding the horse-shoe line of trenches round

St Emilie, with Battalion H.Q. behind the railway embankment between Villers Faucon and St Emilie. A Company of the Somersets was attached to us to help to hold the long length of this salient. They linked up with the Devons on our right, while on our left and considerably to our rear was the 58th Division. We had about one and a half miles of half-dug trench to hold with less than 400 men all told. They were probably the worst sited trenches in France, with no field of fire and not continuous, completely dominated by the German guns at Epehy, who could fire down them, and by snipers who, by crawling through the thistles and broken country on our left rear (and the Alpini were bold snipers and deadly shots), could fire right up some portions of the trench. The salient held by the 74th Division was considerably in advance of the line held by the Australians on our right and by the Londoners on our left, and was quite an unhealthy spot until the Bosche were pushed out of Epehy.

9th September passed fairly quietly until evening, when D Company (Mr Brodie Brown) was sent to reconnoitre to the front, and if possible establish themselves on the ridge on the far side of the valley in front of us. They had got about three quarters of the way when their patrols reported at least two companies of the enemy going into the trenches which D were to occupy and two strong patrols working forward on either side of them. To push on was impossible, so they returned to the trenches they had left. Though this merely confirmed what we already knew - that the enemy were holding that line in strength - and though a report was sent in to this effect, because the Air Force had reported that they could see no signs of the enemy, Corps ordered us to push forward at dawn next morning and occupy the crest of the ridge. These orders were only received at 2 A.M., and though Company Commanders were summoned at once A Company (Sergeant W. Collier) only received his orders at dawn - the runner having missed the way in the dark. The company of Somersets were to attack on the right, keeping touch with the Devons, C Company (Mr I.W. Cruickshank) in the centre, B Company (Mr J. M'Lean) on the left, with D Company (Mr Brodie Brown) in reserve. A Company (Sergeant W. Collier) was to keep in touch with the Londoners (58th Division) on the left and advance in conjunction with them. The time for our barrage opening was postponed, but the wire from Brigade never reached us and we advanced without any preliminary bombardment. C Company and the Somersets almost reached their objectives unobserved when they were met by very heavy machine-gun and rifle fire. B Company on the left were unable to push on which left C Company's left flank exposed. Into this gap the enemy quickly rushed fresh troops and attacked in force with the result that the two companies were overwhelmed by numbers and nearly surrounded. They were ordered to retire but not more than a quarter got back.

We consequently were forced to hold our old line as a defensive line and get liason with the 58th Division, who also found the enemy in great strength and were unable to hold what they gained. We learned afterwards that a regiment (three battalions) of the enemy were holding the line between Ronssoy and Templeux le Guerard with orders to fight to the last. The Battalion was now very exhausted, the trenches were knee-deep in water, and a great number of Lewis guns and rifles were out of action with mud and water. Major D.D. Ogilvie and Mr Brodie Brown were the only officers left in the line, with Mr J.W. Ormiston doing liaison between Battalion H.Q. and Captain R.H. Colthart at Battle H.Q. - telephonic communication was almost impossible as the line was broken every five minutes. We were consequently very pleased when we were told we were to be relieved by the 10th East Kent Regiment (230th Brigade), who took over from us that night and we moved back to Longavenes.

Here we found a draft of twelve Black Watch officers awaiting us, and the day was spent in cleaning ourselves. Next day (12th

September) we moved back to Templeux la Fosse, with Battalion H.Q. in the old Prisoners of War compound and the companies in trenches. Major J.M. M'Kenzie, Royal Scots, arrived to take over command of the Battalion from, Major D.D. Ogilvie, and Brig.-General F.S. Thackeray (H.L.I.) assumed command of the Brigade which Lieut.-Colonel C.J.H. Spence-Jones, Pembroke Yeomanry, had commanded since Brig.-General R. Hoare had been wounded. We had six restful days here and then moved up to Faustine Quarry in reserve for the attack by the Division. A Company (Mr P. Dane) were attached to the Somersets, who had suffered a lot of casualties from gas.

The III. Corps continued the attack on 18th September with a view to securing a position affording good observation on the Hindenburg line. The 1st Australian Division co-operated on our right and the 16th Division on our left. Against us was the 38th Division (German) holding from Templeux le Guerard to Ronssoy.

Our divisional frontage had been reduced by nearly half, each brigade having been responsible for about 1000 yards. The 230th (and the Somersets) were on the right, 231st (with the Devons) on the left, leaving only ourselves in reserve. Aided by a haze and a very effective barrage the attack was a complete success, the first objectives being gained by 7.45 A.M. with very few casualties and a large bag of prisoners. On advancing over the ridge towards the second objective A Company came under very heavy machine-gun fire from Rifleman Post, but our artillery soon silenced that, and we were in occupation of Rifleman Post by one o'clock - an advance of 4500 yards. Here we consolidated, and remained till relieved by the Sussex. A Company's casualties were 4 killed and 25 wounded, and they had a number of prisoners and machine guns to their credit.

20th September was spent in salvage work on the battlefield, and at 10 P.M. we moved forward to relieve the Suffolks at Toine

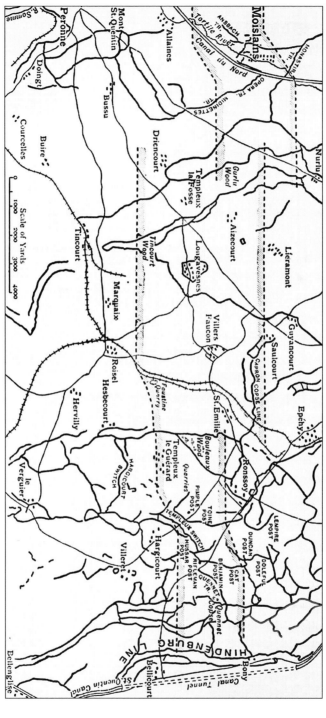

The Divisional Boundaries for the three phases of the advance are shown by shaded lines. The first two advances were on a 1-Brigade frontage, the third on a 2-Brigade frontage with only our Battalion in Reserve. Opposed to us were the Alpine Corps (1st Bavarian Regiment and Body Infantry Regiment), with the 6th Cavalry Division on their right and the 96th and 95th Imperial Regiments of the 38th Division on their left.

MAP SHOWING THE TRENCH SYSTEM ON THE SOMME.

In addition to the principal trenches, use was made of all sunken roads and belts of barbed wire stretched across the country.

and Pimple Posts - the first objectives in the attack. On the 22nd we relieved the 25th R.W.F. in the front line, and held from Carbine Trench to Benjamin Post with A Company in support at Artaxerxes Post. The enemy shelled the position heavily both with high explosives and gas and we suffered some casualties.

The Division was now consolidated on the line of the second objective, and it was obvious that the Bosche were holding the high ground, particularly Quennet Copse and Quennemont Farm, very strongly, and it was impossible for the tired and depleted Division to advance without further preparation. The line held by the enemy was our old front line of March overlooking the Bellicourt-Le Catalet section of the Hindenburg line, and they were determined to hang on to that at all costs. The attack on the Hindenburg line was not for us. The 74th Division was booked for the advance further north.

On the night of the 24/25th September we were relieved by two companies of the 106th American Battalion; got to Faustine Quarry by 5 A.M. and at 8 marched to Tincourt, where we entrained for Villers-Bretonneux. From Villers-Bretonneux we marched to Corbie (fifteen miles east of Amiens) and got into billets there. This was the last we were to see of the Somme, for we were destined for another front. That our services on the Somme front were appreciated is shown by the following letter received by our Division from General Rawlinson, Commanding Fourth Army, dated 28th September:-

"*74th Division*. - The 74th Division has taken a prominent part in the successful advance of the Fourth Army during the past month, and, much to my regret, has been ordered to another part of the British front.

"The work of this Division during a period of severe and continuous fighting is worthy of the best traditions of the yeoman stock of Great Britain.

"Brought to this country from a hot climate, where they took part in a very different method of warfare, the 74th Division has quickly adapted itself to the altered conditions, and has fought with a determination and courage which is beyond praise.

"In the capture of AIZECOURT, DRIENCOURT, TEMPLEUX LA FOSSE, LONGAVESNES, VILLIERS FAUCON, and TEMPLEUX LE GUERARD, the Division has made a name for itself which ranks with the best division fighting in the British Army, and I desire to offer to all ranks my warmest thanks for their gallantry and self-sacrifice.

"In addition to the considerable area of ground gained the Division has captured over 1700 prisoners.

"I greatly regret that the Division is leaving the Fourth Army, and in wishing all ranks every good fortune, I trust I may at some future time find the 74th Division once more under my command."

We left Corbie early in the morning of the 28th for Mericourt where we entrained for Berguette, reaching our destination the following morning, whence we marched to our billeting area in Bourecq, just south of our old billeting ground at Fontes. Here we stayed till 2nd October when we moved by the light railway to "what was Locon." Two days later we were at Herlies. On the night 10/11th October the 229th Brigade took over from the 231st Brigade, and on the 14th we moved into the line relieving the 12th Battalion S.L.I., D Company on left, A in centre, and B on right, with C in support in Ligny Wood. On 15th October we occupied the railway line east of Ligny, and next day our patrols had pushed forward to the outskirts of Haubourdin (a suburb of Lille). On the 17th we again advanced, crossed the Haute Deule Canal, and on reaching our final objective handed over to the 16th Devons while we remained in support. Petit Ronchin, Ascq (on the Lille-

Tournai road), and Baisieux gave us billets for the following nights. We were now in support to the Somersets, who carried on the advance until held up outside Marquain. The 231st Brigade had been withdrawn, so the Division was advancing on a one-battalion frontage.

As soon as Orcq was gained we were to pass through the Somersets and carry on the advance. The enemy's resistance, however, was stiffening, and the Somersets were unable to push on. On the 22nd we took over the line in front of Orcq, but found it impossible to patrol much to the front owing to the heavy machine-gun fire. The trenches opposite were well wired in and strongly manned, and the attack by B Company on the 23rd was held up within 100 yards of the objective by intense trench-mortar and machine-gun fire and artillery barrage, and the two platoons were compelled to withdraw to their original line after suffering 32 casualties.

Next day we were relieved by the 10th Buffs and moved back to billets in Baisieux, where we rested for ten days and got through an inter-platoon football competition. On the evening of 1st November the enemy put over a few shells, and in going to regulate the traffic into the cellars Captain R.H. Colthart was mortally wounded. The death of our adjutant was a great loss to the Battalion. As Sergeant Colthart he had gone out with the Regiment to Gallipoli, was appointed quartermaster and then adjutant, and had been with the Regiment or Battalion in every engagement in which it had taken part, being mentioned in dispatches. Lieutenant J.W. Ormiston succeeded him as adjutant.

Tournai was evacuated by the Germans on 9th November. The 231st Brigade promptly passed through it, and formed a bridgehead east of the town with the 55th Division on their right and the 57th Division on the left. The 230th Brigade occupied the town while we moved forward to Lamain. Next day we marched through Tournai, and had a tremendous reception. The skirl of the pipes and the sight of the kilts moved the population to great enthusiasm, both vocal and osculatory, and we had a regular triumphal procession. Our destination was Beclers, five miles east of Tournai.

On 11th November we were continuing our advance east, and had reached the main road just west of Frasnes, when at twenty minutes before 11 o'clock the Brigade-Major (Captain A.J.M. Tuck, M.C.) informed us that an armistice had been signed which came in force at 11 o'clock. The consequent halt threw our time-table out of gear, and we finally stumbled in to our billeting area in the dark, covered with mud and very weary.

The following day our Brigade relieved the 230th Brigade in holding the outpost line, and we were billeted at Izieres. The inhabitants could not do too much for us, and we were quite sorry when orders were received on the 17th to proceed to Moustier. We had been transferred back again into the Fifth Army. Here we rubbed up our ceremonial drill and practised guard of honour for the King's visit. This, however, fell through, and on the 7th December we marched to a point on the Leuze-Tournai road, near Barry, where His Majesty held an informal inspection.

While at Moustier we started elementary educational training, which was more fully developed after we moved to Grammont on 16th December. Here our wanderings finally ceased, and demobilization commenced. We had a most successful and sumptuous dinner on Christmas Day, the whole N.-E. of France having been ransacked for geese and turkeys. On New Year's Day Lieut.-Colonel J.M. M'Kenzie went home sick, and Major D.D. Ogilvie assumed command. Educational training in the forenoon and sports in the afternoon was the order of the day, and everyone looked forward to demobilization and Blighty once more.

After defeating the K.S.L.I, in the semi-final we met the M.G.C. in the final for the Divisional Cup on 22nd January, whom we beat 3-0. Considering we had only four of the original team left it was all the more creditable that we managed to pull it off. Major-

THE BATTALION FOOTBALL TEAM.

Standing (left to right.) - Sgt. Patterson, 2ⁿᵈ Lt. Gourlay, Pte. Davidson, Pte. Buchanan, Pte. Thomson, Sgt. Fyall, Pte. Gair.

Sitting - Sgt. Goodall, Lt.-Col. Ogilvie, Pte. M'Guffog, Cpl. Davis, Capt. Andrew.

In front - Pte. Petrie, Pte. Moir.

123

General E.S. Girdwood, C.B., presented a very beautiful silver cup and medals to the winning team, and Battalion medals were also sent to all members of the team. For the Divisional Cup our record was: - Played 6: won 5: drawn 1: goals for 25: goals against 6. Unfortunately a complete record of the Regimental and Battalion team was not kept, but we have records of the last 74 matches. Of these 66 were won: 3 lost: 5 drawn: goals for 217: goals against 45.

The Divisional Cross Country Run was also won by us, and we were selected to run in the Inter-Corps Run. One or two successful mule gymkhanas were got up, and we also tried our hand at baseball, cricket, and paper chases, both mounted and on foot. Two or three nights a week we had dances, and one or two good concert parties entertained us.

Each week we kept sending men off for demobilization, and about the third week in March we sent about 100 men to the 8th Battalion the Black Watch, and half a dozen officers to the 6th Battalion in the Army of the Rhine. This reduced us to cadre strength. On 18th June the cadre consisting of 2 officers and 22 other ranks proceeded home via Boulogne, and a few days later the baggage guard followed, after handing over all Battalion stores at Dunkirk. Of those who went out on the *Andania* only four remained - Lieut.-Colonel D.D. Ogilvie, Captain R.A. Andrew, M.C., R.Q.M.S. W.J. Galbraith and Sergeant-Major W. Nisbet. The cadre reached Kirkcaldy on 25th June, where they were entertained by the Provost on behalf of the Corporation, and in the afternoon were all demobilized at Kinross.

So ends the history of the 14th (Fife and Forfar Yeomanry) Battalion, the Black Watch, Royal Highlanders.

On 6th September 1915 Lord Lovat received the following wire from Windsor Castle: -

"I send you and your Brigade my best wishes on your departure for Active Service. I feel sure that the great and traditional fighting reputation of Scotsmen will be more than

safe with you, and that your Brigade will spare no effort in the interests of the Empire's cause to bring this war to a victorious conclusion.

GEORGE R.I. "

The purport of this short history is to show how we did our best to carry out His Majesty's command.

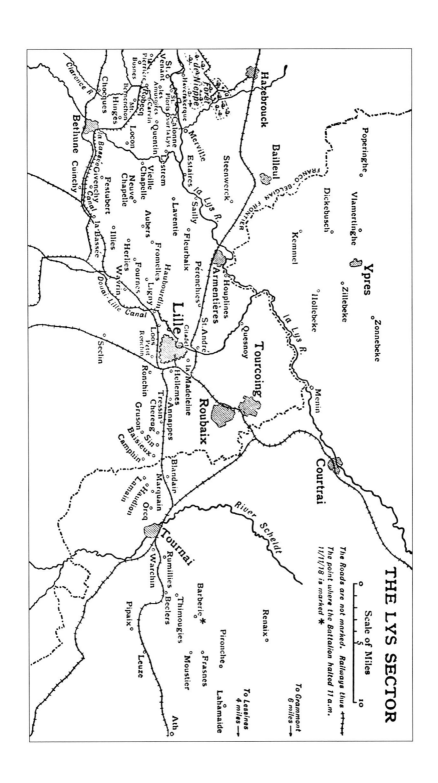

THE LYS SECTOR

Scale of Miles

0   5   10

The Roads are not marked. Railways thus
The point where the Battalion halted 11 a.m.
11/11/18 is marked ✱

To Grammont
6 miles →

To Lessines
4 miles →

Poperinghe

Vlamertinghe

Dickebusch

Ypres

Zillebeke

Zonnebeke

Hollebeke

Kemmel

Menin

Ypres

Hazebrouck

Bailleul

FRANCO-BELGIAN FRONTIER

la Lys R.

Steenwerck

Merville

Forêt de Nieppe

Havrenkerque

Floris sur la Lys

Calonne

St. Venant

Estaires

Sailly

Fleurbaix

Lavente

Armentières

Houplines

Pérenchies

St. André

Quesnoy

la Lys R.

Tourcoing

Courtrai

River Scheldt

Bethune

Clarence R.

Chocques

Busnes

Robecq

Hinges

Berguenchen

Locon

Mt. Bernenchon

la Bassée

Givenchy

Canal

la Bassée

Canal

Festubert

Neuve Chapelle

Vieille Chapelle

Quentin

Lestrem

Aubers

Fromelles

Herlies

Fournes

Ligny

Haubourdin

Loos

Petit Ronchin

Lille

Illies

Wavrin

Fournes

Douai-Lille Canal

Seclin

Citadel

la Madeleine

Hellemes

Ronchin

Roubaix

Tressin

Annappes

Chereng

Gruson

Sin

Baisieux

Camphin

Blandain

Marquain

Lamain

Orcq

Haudion

Tournai

Watchin

Rumillies

Beclers

Pipaix

Leuze

Ath

Renaix

Barberie ✱

Thimougies

Moustier

Pironche

Frasnes

Lahamaide

- CHAPTER VII -
SOME PERSONALITIES

IN WRITING THIS SHORT history of the regiment I have carefully abstained from all personalities. These few notes on some of our best known characters are only added to recall pleasant - or other - memories, and the subjects are asked to forgive the liberty taken.

To criticise one's superiors is both impolitic and impertinent, but there are three who cannot be omitted - two of them live in England and may never see this book, and the third - well, he has expressed his opinion of me quite bluntly more than once already.

At Grammont I received a letter from a very well-known member of the football team thanking me for the medals, in which he said: - "We always liked General Girdwood for his kindly consideration for the men, and I know I am only expressing the opinion of all the boys when I say we would not have changed him for Haig himself." There is no doubt that was the opinion of the whole Division about our G.O.C. - and, fortunately, we only had the one. Whether he was talking to the men after a good bit of work in the line, or at a formal inspection in the "back area," one always felt how keenly interested he was in the men. They loved his "Beatty" cap - but not his roasts of beef. He always expressed his appreciation of good work, but apparently disliked the growing of oats on the spare pole of one of the limbers - but the transport know more about that than I do!

The G.O.C. had certainly a brain-wave when he adopted the "Broken Spur" as our Divisional badge. We were all very proud of our "Broken Spur." An Australian officer, seeing it at Faustine

Quarry, asked if it was the badge of the 74th Division. "Well," he added, "we call you 'Allenby's Harriers,' because you are the only Division we can't keep up with." Coming from an Australian that was "some" praise.

I don't know which was the more popular - the G.O.C. or "Reggie."[1] But "Reggie" took some knowing, and though it was capital fun watching him strafing others - which he did "full out" - it was quite another thing when he turned his guns on you! He was a tremendous sportsman, and it didn't seem to matter whether he was hunting sentries or jackal - so long as he was hunting he was quite happy - while the feelings of the sentry and the jackal were also probably similar! He took a tremendous pride in the Brigade - "I take off my hat every time to the 229th" - and I fancy what pleased him far more than defeating Turk or Bosche was our victory over the Scots Guards at Grand Roullecourt.

If we had gone abroad within three months after mobilization nothing would have saved "Black Mick"[2] - if within six months it was about even odds. At nine months all the N.C.O.'s, a good many of the men, and even one or two subalterns might have tried to save him; while after a year, if any one had dared to lay hands on him, he would have been rent in twain by the entire Regiment. And the reason was obvious. Realising what capital material he had to deal with, Mick was determined that, whatever people might think of him, his job was to get the Regiment to the highest state of efficiency in the shortest possible time. The pill certainly was a bit bitter, and it was only when the effects began to be felt that we realised what a thundering good Doctor "Mick" was. Shortly before we went out he admitted that we were as good as any cavalry regiment in the Army, but characteristically added - "but don't tell the —!"

1. Brigadier-General R. Hoare, C.M.G., D.S.O.
2. Capt. (later Lieut.-Col.) M.E. Lindsay, D.S.O., 7th D.G.

A very effective combination were the Colonel and Mick, and if we didn't love them much at the time we realise now how much we owe them.

Subalterns and N.C.O.'s were to Mick as a bone to a puppy - he could chew us as much as he liked to-day, but we were still there for similar treatment on the morrow! But how pleased we were when his big black horse played up one day and knocked his cap off!

His language was pointed and all-embracing, and our ancestry and morals both seemed to meet with his disapproval. It is therefore impossible to give any anecdote about Mick. When the narrator's opinion of Mick is added to Mick's opinion of the narrator, the story could only be told in Russian. "Always have an answer ready," was his advice, "even if it isn't the truth - like Mr Sharp's answer just now."

Sharpie[3] and Ralph Stewart were quite the best at looking after themselves, and carried more gear than all the rest of us put together. At Syderstone Common an inquisitive general ordered the tarpaulin to be taken off the General Service wagon, and the first things which caught his eye were Sharpie's tennis racket and golf clubs. At Gara munitions of war had to be left behind to find room on the truck for his patent washstand. By the time he got to Palestine Johnnie Smith really could not compete with his belongings, and had to "borrow" a donkey to carry what could not possibly be left at Cox's Go-down - and it took eight months after the Armistice was signed before sufficient shipping could be collected at Alexandria to bring that home.

"Tukie"[4] and "Doctor" Ross[5] of course go together - I don't know which had the more character.

---

3. Capt. H.S. Sharp.

4. Capt. A.L. Tuke, M.C., R.A.M.C.(T.).

5. Cpl. (later Sgt.) A.J. Ross, M.M., R.A.M.C., attd. F. and F.Y. and 14th R.H.

"What's the guid o' gaen tae oor Doctor? He wadna believe yer ill till yer deid, and he wadna believe yer deid till yer stinkin." Scrimshankers got little sympathy from either. "I've got awful pains in my back, Doctor," said one man, and a knowing look passed between the Doctor and Ross. "Off with your shirt then." A good old smack on his bare back and - "that's all right, my man. A good dose of castor oil, Corporal Ross. Medicine and duty."

Corporal Ross was a wonderful detective. He knew the past history and character of every man in the Regiment, I am sure. Though no two could have taken more care over you when you were really sick than Tukie and his corporal, no two were harder on anyone they knew was shamming. How these two worked on Gallipoli! Finally Tukie had to give in and was literally pushed on board a hospital ship, but he was as bad as a patient as he was good as a doctor, and they were glad to get rid of him at Malta after a short time and return him to his beloved Unit. Egypt, of course, afforded great scope for Tukie's fly-extermination crusade, and I have already referred in the text to his extraordinary success in exterminating mosquitoes at Sherika.

In Palestine his sanitary schemes were almost universally adopted, and his award of a Military Cross hardly represents the great improvements he introduced into the sanitation and health of the Force. We were all very sorry to lose Tukie, but realised that his ability was wasted as a regimental doctor, and felt he was better employed at the citadel where he had more opportunity of using his great surgical powers. We only hope he didn't drop cigarette ash into the interiors of his patients.

Others we lost far too soon were Ronnie Hutchison, O.C. Machine Gun Section, who went to the M.G.C. His favourite word of command was "Gallop," and his joy to jump ditches and hedges with his carts; Pat Rigg and David Marshall, also Machine Gunners; Willie Don, who had to leave us in Egypt owing to heart trouble. His Grace of Canterbury himself could not have intoned words of command more melodiously than Willie did. Charlie Herdman, our finest exponent of horsemanship. He left us in Egypt to go to Remounts, and there he was absolutely in his element, horse, camel, and donkey-coping. Spreull the Vet., who went to the R.A.V.C. in France. Nor is anyone likely to forget "Daddy" Ricketts, the Q.M., if he ever tried to extract anything from his stores, or Gervase Babington (family motto "What is thine is mine") if he happened to possess anything Gervase or his troop coveted.

"Ackety-ack"[6] - otherwise Willie Campbell - had one great failing. He could see no farther than A Squadron or A Company, and if anyone ran down "A" he foamed at the mouth. Ask him how many sergeants there were in No. 1 platoon - which won one of the inter-platoon football competitions - and he was abusive for a week! "Ackety" was perhaps seen at his best playing for the officers' team. On the advice of the crowd, "Go for the man, sir, never mind the ball," he invariably went for Collier or Herd or Dommett, the adjutant of the Somersets - each one quite two or more stone heavier than himself. He and "Aeroplane"[7] were well matched, nothing striking to look at but grand stayers. Willie was due for leave about the first week of January 1919, but as he had spent all his money, and about £200 of other people's, on the men's Christmas dinner, he had just to stay where he was from want of funds to take him home.

While at Sherika, Ross Robertson left us to join R.F.C. He was our first signal officer, and when he left was second in command B Squadron. We lost in Rossie a very capable and popular officer, and his death on his first solo over the German lines at Cambrai was keenly felt by the entire Regiment. Morning stables were of no interest to Rossie - all the energy he could raise was devoted to

---

6. Capt. (later Major) Sir W.A.A. Campbell, Bart., M.C.

7. His charger.

flicking the heads off the daisies in his lines, but give him a definite job to do and no one could do it better.

Unlike his successor, nothing could worry him - Bill Scott, on the other hand, took his telephones very seriously. Till the day he went home we pulled his leg about his 'phones. Ormy,[8] in particular, being lavish in advice as to what to do, and threatening to get Jock Clark if he (Scott) couldn't do it.

Ormy was a great fellow. The less he knew about a subject, the more advice he would give and would argue the point *ad nauseam*. He was reading Law at the time - perhaps that is why.

Perhaps "Dinkum's"[9] best *bon mot* was when he nicknamed M'Dougal[10] the "Gallipoli Spider," and Mac certainly had a wonderful knack of gathering all things into his web. Gallipoli gave him splendid opportunity for his Autolycus-like habits, and rumour has it that, though really ill with dysentery, he took off with him from Suvla seventeen ground sheets and nearly as many blankets. At Sherika, rather than lose his share of the ice, he took it with his tea.

Bombing was his strong point, and as an instructor in hand and rifle grenades he was first class. Routine he hated like poison. Mac is perhaps the only officer who was witty once - and only once - in his trench report. I don't know if H.Q. see the point of his remarks to this day. He it was, who, having overshot the mark, and lost his way in Palestine, was shown back to our lines by a Turkish officer!

"George Washington," Cummins,[11] "lost his nerve," so he said, through being mauled by a lion in South Africa. This is purely supposition on his part, as he had no notion what nerves were. We sometimes wondered if he even knew what pain was. He was badly

---

8. Lieut. (A/Capt.) J.W. Ormiston.

9. Pte. Henderson, B Squadron.

10. Lieut. (later Capt.) A.R. M'Dougal.

11. Lieut. (late Capt.) W.W. Cummins.

frost-bitten on Suvla, and had to be pushed off the Peninsula - at Sheria a bullet passed through his forearm and grazed his upper arm and ribs. He got it tied up, and continued with the advance, and then assisted wounded all night at the dressing-station. The C.O. ordered him to go to the Field Ambulance at once to have his wound seen to, but George put in four more hours before complying with the order.

At Fakenham an officer joined us from the Wild West - a cow-puncher and lassoo expert. The obvious name for him was Arizona;[12] and Arizona he remained. I have even heard him referred to as Captain Arizona. An enthusiast in whatever he took up, he was in turn scout officer, transport officer, Lewis gun officer, quartermaster and company commander. But it is as sports officer that he will be best remembered - training the football or running teams, coaching the tug-of-war, organising cricket or baseball, or arranging mule gymkhanas or swimming matches. One of his best efforts was coaching the tug-of-war team in the final against Lovats at Sohag. Only when his handkerchief was in his right hand were his instructions "genuine."[13] - "Heave" with it in his left meant nothing, and completely mystified the opposing coach. Poor old Arizona! He went out with us to Gallipoli, and was with us to the very end. Shortly after coming home he had an operation on his broken nose, and everything seemed all right, but pleuritic pneumonia set in, and he died very suddenly in a nursing home in St Andrews in February of this year.

There is one officer about whom innumerable stories could be told - no need to mention his name. He, it was who, looking through a periscope, well below the parapet, waved to a Turkish deserter to come in, and could not understand how the Turk didn't see him.

---

12. Lieut. (late Capt.) R.A. Andrew, M.C.

13. Pronounced "genu-*eine.*"

When he was mounting his horse one day it collapsed and died on the spot.

"That's a funny thing, Sergeant Cooper; I've never known this horse do that before."

"Will you take my punishment or go before a court-martial?" "Your award, Sir."

"Well, go away, and don't do it again!"

When asked how he got on when torpedoed on the way home, all we learnt from him was, "It was very wet."

Then there is the oft quoted, "What are you complaining about? It's only another five miles, and you've cocoa for your tea!"

Mac Lindsay,[14] the stock-whip expert and jack-of-all-trades, confessed to only one ambition in life - to dress - in a little red jacket and fez and lead him round on a chain! The report that he made a Ford car out of bully-beef tins has, I understand, been officially denied.

Just a week before the Armistice we lost Colthart, the best quartermaster in the Army, and one of the best of fellows. He had a wonderful "way with him," and could get for us all sorts of stores, etc., which other quartermasters were unable to get. He was with us all the time, and never missed a "show."

Colthart once "took pity" on a stray donkey in Palestine. Government oats soon made a tremendous difference, and the donkey was sold at Yalo for, I think, £11. Unfortunately, the previous owner met the new purchaser with the donkey, and all explanations being unavailing, a court of enquiry was the result, to which witnesses seemed to come from all over Palestine. Eventually, the donkey was returned to its previous owner, and all parties satisfied - except the donkey.

Dick Wood and Harry Fraser were two of the best we got from the Black Watch. Dick Wood looked benevolent enough behind his

---

14. Lieut. A.S. Lindsay, M.B.E., M.C.

spectacles, but in a scrap his lust for blood was insatiable. Harry's penchant was stalking Bosche machine gun posts. Unfortunately, he got it badly in the neck just as success was at hand, and was away from us till about the Armistice.

He and the other Harry (Adamson) looked after the transport lines. Arizona told Harry Adamson to take his platoon forward and see if the Bosche were still holding their trenches on the Lys Sector. "Hairy's" method was typical of the man. Thinking it might be a "dirty" job, "Hairy" left his platoon under cover and went on himself. Having failed to find any Bosche in their trenches, he got up on the parapet and waved to his platoon to come on!

Of the N.C.O.'s and men it is possible only to mention a few.

I always associate S.M. Alec. Ogilvie with Hogsthorpe at early morning stand-to going round the lines, abusing everyone for making a noise, and himself making as much noise as all the rest of us put together. He was the life and soul of C Squadron. Heaven knows what C would have done without him on the Peninsula. He and Edie and M'Laren, our three squadron sergeant-majors, were a very strong trio. Edie was an example to all of us - however tired he might be himself he never thought of resting till he was satisfied his men were all right.

One man, I know, will never forget Sergeant Craig (he was made R.Q.M.S. just a few days before his death on Suvla). Craig found lice "doing squaderron drrrill up his legs," and he was pegged out in an outhouse till his clothes were fumigated.

S.M. Bradfield was another splendid fellow who lost his life - the result of frost bite - on Gallipoli. Corporal "One 'wo" was a physical instructor in civil life, and no one could twist one better at "jerks" than he could.

Then there was the one and only Jock Lumsden. Regularly once a week at morning stables he turned the whole troop out to water, while he and "Dinkum" swept the entire garage out - a sure sign that the previous night had been pay night. He always was a hard worker, but a perfect demon for work the morning after the night before. A squadron leader was showing a man how to use a pick, cutting trenches in the sandstone at Sherika. Up strolled Jock - hands deep in his pockets. "Here, Sergeant-major - this man hasn't the foggiest notion how to use a pick. I've just been showing him." "I've been watching ye, sir. I'm thinking it wad need tae be war time for you to earn ten shillings a day in the pits."

"How many men in this bay for rum, Sergeant Lumsden?" "Four men and myself, sir. That will be nine." When handed his tot, he looked at the bottom of the mug, and handed it back to the orderly sergeant, "Hoots, Gorrie, dinna mak a fule o' my stamach."

An inveterate gambler, but a great sportsman, no one could have been more loyal to his Company than Jock.

When a man on manoeuvres crawls up to a ditch within twenty yards of a very wide awake post, leaves his cap just showing above the bank, and then proceeds up the ditch so as to get within five yards of the sentry, and could only be dislodged from there by stones, one spots him at once as a keen, hard-working fellow. Such was Private Gall, who eventually became R.S.M. He taught us to bayonet fight with "dash, vigour, and determination," and gave us Irish songs and recitations at our smokers.

Another star performer was Craig of the Machine Gun Battery, with his whistling and patter. He eventually got a commission (and the D.S.O.) in the Grenadier Guards.

Then there was Sergeant Renton - who, though badly frost-bitten, refused to leave the front line, and always showed his other foot to the Doctor. He could only hobble with the help of spades as crutches. Young Roger who "saw red" in the Dere and nearly bayonetted the Doctor. Hastie Young, an "old soldier," the regimental barber: he cut the Brig.'s hair, until the Brig. unfortunately ran into Hastie holiday-making in Jerusalem.

Lowson who snored quite happily within a few yards of the Turkish machine gunner at "Amulree"[15] and finally got lost, and "fetched up among the 'Duffs,' I think ye ca' them" (it is as the "Buffs" that they are generally known)!

S.-M. Elder, an old Black Watch man, who when asked if he were dead stoutly denied it.

Little Batchelor, the runner, never flurried and always so polite, however nasty the Bosche might be, was nearly kidnapped by the Australians as a mascot.

"Honest John" M'Niven who would work twenty-four hours a day to make A Company more comfortable.

S.M. Hair whose wonderful pronunciation of words of command always amused us. His "Stind at —ice" electrified everyone; unlike poor old Aitken, whose staccato and rapid "Company company 'shun'" was never heard by anyone! And then the footballers Savage, Herd, Collier (who commanded "hauf a Batt-al-i-on" at St Emilie); Todd, M'Guffog (who captained the team that won the Final of the Divisional Cup, with a bit of Turkish shrapnel so close to his spine that they dared not operate); Davis with a heart like a lion and a kick like a mule; M'Lean who could head the ball about as far as he could kick it; Durham who seemed always half asleep and too lazy to worry - and many another first-rate footballer.

Leitch, the biggest and strongest man we had, the end man of the tug-of-war team, one of our best Lewis gunners, who, when shot in the hand, so that he could not fire his gun, carried on bringing up ammunition boxes all that day.

Henderson, D Coy's S.M.; Galbraith on whom descended Colthart's wonderful knack of obtaining whatever he wanted; Storrer Mosh alias Morrison Storrar of A Squadron and A Coy.

---

15. Amurieh, an isolated hill held by the Turks, raided by the Ayrs and Lanarks, 22nd March 1917.

Mack, one of the best we got from the 10th Battalion, and they were all good fellows; Corporal Gibb, who looked the part so well that he was appointed Acting Q.M.S. by the Stores Officer at Kantara!

And Many More.

Names and episodes crowd one another out - the more one writes, the more one recalls. These random jottings, however, will call up many more to the reader's memory. Such is my hope - that, having started you in a reminiscent frame of mind you will now carry on "spinning the yarn" yourself.

"Here's tae oorsel's! Wha's like us! Damned few!"

THE FIFE AND FORFAR IMPERIAL YEOMANRY AT ANNSMUIR.

- CHAPTER VIII -

THE PREDECESSORS OF THE FIFE AND FORFAR YEOMANRY

DURING THE TROUBLOUS TIMES in France at the end of the eighteenth century the fear of invasion was as acute as it was during the first years of the European War. To meet this danger Pitt issued his famous appeal, and towards the end of 1793 the first yeomanry regiment was raised in Suffolk. Others quickly followed, and in 1794 we find a regiment was raised in Forfar called the Forfar Yeomanry or Angus Cavalry, which continued twenty-five years until disbanded in 1819.

In Fife the first unit raised appears to have been a regiment of "Fencible Cavalry" named "The Fifeshire Light Dragoons"; like other Fencible Units throughout the country this regiment seems to have been more or less a Regular Unit enlisted for the period of the war and for home service only. It was apparently the force on which the Government relied for keeping a check on local unrest, and was disbanded in 1797.

In 1798 the Fife Yeomanry Cavalry and the Stirlingshire Yeomanry Cavalry were raised, and later on Perthshire, Clackmannanshire, and Kinross-shire all had their yeomanry regiments, which, however, seldom exceeded 150 in strength.

In Fife, however, thanks to the inspiration and energy of Sir William Erskine and Mr Wemyss of Cuttlehill, it was very popular; and when the Earl of Crawford was appointed Colonel Commandant in September 1798 there were already seven mounted troops.

DETACHMENT AT H.M. THE KING'S VISIT TO EDINBURGH.

REGIMENTAL DRILL AT ANNSMUIR WITH SKELETON ENEMY.

With change of name to the Royal Fifeshire Yeomanry Cavalry, and under the successive command of Lieut.-Colonel Morison of Naughton (1803), Colonel J. Anstruther Thomson of Charlton (1809), and Colonel W. Wemyss (1823) the Regiment continued to flourish, receiving in 1814 - the year which saw the close of the war - the thanks of both Houses of Parliament for its services.

In 1822 the Regiment took part in the Review held by His Majesty King George IV. on Portobello sands where, according to a contemporary account, "the novelty of an exhibition of this order, and the passion allowable of the ladies to see their gallant and rustic lords and lovers relinquishing the habiliments of common life and flourishing in scarlet and glory, produced an immense crowd."

In December 1827 an Order was circulated announcing the disbandment of many yeomanry regiments, and among those on the list was The Royal Fife. Arms were returned to store, and the Regiment actually disbanded in 1828. The Perthshire, Clackmannanshire, and Kinross-shire Yeomanries were also disbanded at this time.

The troublous times of 1830 reached their height in the winter of that year, and many yeomanry regiments were re-established, amongst them being the Fifeshire Yeomanry Cavalry, commanded by General Balfour of Balbirnie. The Regiment was again disbanded in 1838, the same fate overcoming the Stirlingshire Yeomanry.

In 1856 the Forfar Yeomanry were re-raised, and in 1860 the Fifeshire Mounted Rifle Volunteers, under command of Lieut.-General The Earl of Rosslyn, Captain Anstruther Thomson, son of the officer who had commanded the Fife Yeomanry and Fife Fencible Cavalry half a century before, Captain Whyte Melville of the 9th Lancers, Captain Oswald of the Grenadier Guards, son of Captain Oswald of Dunnikier of the Royal Rifles, and Captain Sir Arthur Halkett, who had carried the colours of the 42nd Royal Highlanders at the Battle of the Alma, were the Troop leaders.

Though the Regiment was only officially accepted in June, they were present at the Royal Review in Edinburgh in September, marching past Her Majesty The Queen in rear of the Scots Greys.

In 1862 the Forfar Yeomanry were disbanded, and for the next fourteen years there were no Yeomanry in Forfarshire.

In 1870, on the application of Lieut.-Colonel Anstruther Thomson, the Mounted Rifle Volunteers were turned into Light Horse, and the Corps was called the 1st Fifeshire Volunteer Light Horse Corps, with an establishment of 240 all ranks.

Towards the end of 1875 a movement was made to raise a Forfarshire Troop of Light Horse, and early in 1876 a strong Troop, known as the 1st Forfarshire Light Horse Volunteer Corps, was raised at Dundee under command of Captain P.A.W. Carnegy of Lour and attached to the Fife Light Horse.

In 1895 Lieut.-Colonel John Gilmour of Montrave succeeded to the command of the Regiment, and introduced the Squadron System - "A" Squadron having its headquarters at Cupar, "B" Squadron at Dunfermline, and the "Forfar" Squadron at Dundee.

In October 1899 the South African War broke out, and early in 1900 the 20th Company Imperial Yeomanry was formed. Captain Chappell Hodge, late 12th Lancers, was given command, and under him were Lieutenants J. Gilmour and J. Simpson. They embarked on 27th February for Cape Town where they were given their horses, and proceeded to join General Sir A. Hunter's Division for the relief of Mafeking. The "Fifes" crossing the Vaal captured the town of Christiana in the Transvaal - the first act of war on Transvaal soil.

After the death of Captain Hodge, Captain R. Purvis took command till wounded at Nooitgedacht, when Lieutenant J. Gilmour succeeded him.

In May 1901 the first contingent, after having marched 2575 miles and taken part in 85 engagements, proceeded home.

The 20th Company Imperial Yeomanry continued to serve till the end of the war, receiving in all 498 officers and men from the Fife and Forfar Light Horse.

The conversion of the Light Horse into Imperial Yeomanry took place in 1901, and the Regiment then became the Fife and Forfar Imperial Yeomanry - in 1908, on the formation of the Territorial Force, the word "Imperial" was dropped.

In 1901 Lieut.-Colonel Sir John Gilmour retired and was succeeded by Lieut.-Colonel T.H. Erskine of Grangemuir, the present Honorary Colonel of the Regiment.

On the outbreak of war in 1914 the Regiment was commanded by Lieut.-Colonel A. Mitchell of Luscar, subsequent Commanding Officers being Lieut.-Colonels J. Gilmour, J. Younger, J.M. M'Kenzie, and D.D. Ogilvie. During this period the Adjutants were Captains M.E. Lindsay, H.S. Sharp, A.C. Smith, W.D. Brown, R. Colthart, and J.W. Ormiston.

GROUP SHOWING SIX SUCCESSIVE COMMANDING OFFICERS.
Standing (left to right) - Lt. Younger, Capt. Lumsden, Lt. Stewart, Capt. Haig, Col. Anstruther Thomson, Lt. Russell, Lt. Wright (Yorkshire Dragoons), Lt. Nairn, Capt. Dewar. Sitting - Major Osborne, Major Gilmour, Major Mitchell, Major Erskine, Lt.-Col. Sir J. Gilmour, Capt. Burgoyne (Adjutant), Major Marshall, Major Lawson.

THE CADRE ON ARRIVAL AT KIRKCALDY.
(See page 124)

APPENDIX

HONOURS AND AWARDS

D.S.O.

Lieut.-Col. John Gilmour.
Lieut.-Col. James Younger.

M.C.

Capt. Ian Couper Nairn.
Capt. Sir William A.A. Campbell, Bart.
Capt. A.L.S. Tuke, R.A.M.C.(T.).
Lieut. Robert A. Andrew.
2nd Lieut. Alec C. Smith.
2nd Lieut. William Jeffrey Johnstone.
2nd Lieut. John Crawford Houston.
2nd Lieut. A. Richard Wood. D.C.M., M.M.
2nd Lieut. T. Brodie Brown.
345626 C.S.M. John Cameron.

D.C.M.

131 S.S.M. Alexander Ogilvie.
345018 C.S.M. William Henderson.
345416 Sergt. William Collier.
345200 Sergt. William Syme.

345314 Sergt. William R. Chalmers.

1437 L/Sergt. J. Valentine.

290604 Private James Birrell.

345094 Private H.A. Dickie.

2029 Private W. Roger.

345209 Private Thomas Spence.

M.M.

345674 Sergt. Alex. Park Gordon.

345375 Sergt. William Herd.

345380 Sergt. James Johnston.

345749 Cpl. J. Black.

300005 Cpl. Alexander J. Ross, R.A.M.C.

345074 L/Cpl. John J. Leitch.

345320 L/Cpl. E. Lippiatt.

345409 L/Cpl. A. Sinclair.

345116 L/Cpl. David Maxwell Telfer.

11463 Private J. Armour.

16877 Private Alex. Black. D.C.M.

345446 Private William Blair.

345259 Private A. Campbell.

26870 Private Richard Izatt.

345075 Private Douglas Rodger.

345740 Private W.T. Smith.

M.S.M.

345141 R.S.M. George Call.

345166 C.S.M. John Skinner Lumsden.

345191 R.Q.M.S. William James Galbraith.

345021 C.Q.M.S. William Blyth.
345095 C.Q.M.S. John M'Niven.

SERBIAN GOLD MEDAL

2025 S.S. D.H. Pringle.

ITALIAN BRONZE MEDAL

345031 L/Cpl. Alexander Wilson.

MEDAILLE BARBATIE SI CREDINTA - 1ST CLASS

345426 Sergt. Robert Ballantyne.

MENTION IN DISPATCHES

Lieut.-Col. John Gilmour.
Major James Younger.
Major Cecil George de Prée.
Capt. Michael E. Lindsay.
Capt. D. Douglas Ogilvie.
Capt. Sir William A.A. Campbell, Bart.
Lieut. David Colville.
Lieut. Henry Adamson.
2nd Lieut. Alec C. Smith.
2nd Lieut. A.S. Lindsay.
Lieut. (A/Capt.) Robert Herd Colthart.
Lieut. Robert A. Andrew.

2nd Lieut. (A/Capt.) John W. Ormiston.

131 S.S.M. Alexander Ogilvie.

977 S.Q.M.S. J. Edmund.

345113 Sergt. Alex. Sievewright.

345185 Sergt. William Scott.

345424 Sergt. D. Low.

345943 Sergt. Duncan Campbell.

792 Sergt. Nathaniel Mack.

1860 L/Sergt. James R. Barron.

345165 L/Sergt. R.M. Hogg.

345476 Cpl. William A. Milne.

650 Cpl. Alex. J. Ross, R.A.M.C.

345245 L/Cpl. J. Brown.

345302 L/Cpl. John Clark.

345031 L/Cpl. Alexander Wilson.

345180 Private Thomas Blease.

345154 Private William Dunn.

345052 Private Frederick Paterson.

CERTIFICATES OF GALLANTRY

1860 Cpl. James Barron.

1826 Private James Benton.

1851 Private James Salmond.

2441 Private W. Whyte.

HONOURS GAINED BY OFFICERS EXTRA REGIMENTALLY EMPLOYED

Lieut.-Col. Alex. J. King, C.M.G. D.S.O.

Lieut.-Col. Andrew Spreull, R.A.V.C. D.S.O.

Major George Erskine Jackson. O.B.E., M.C.
Major (A/Lt.-Col.) Ronald G.O. Hutchison. D.S.O., M.C.
Capt. Harold S. Sharp. Mention.
Capt. Charles W. Herdman. Mention.
Capt. Harold W.V. Temperley. O.B.E.
Capt. A.S. Lindsay, M.B.E. M.C., Croix de Guerre.
Capt. David Marshall. M.C.
Lieut. R. Warburton. M.C.
Lieut. A.G. Brown. M.C.
Lieut. W.J. Rae. M.C.

HONOURS GAINED BY FORMER ADJUTANTS

Colonel (Hon. Brig.-Gen.) M.L. MacEwen,
    C.B. Legion d'Honneur.
Lieut.-Col. (Hon. Brig.-Gen.) G.R.H. Cheape,
    C.M.G. D.S.O., M.C.
Lieut.-Col. E.C. Jury, C.M.G. M.C.
Major (Temp. Lieut.-Col.) M.E. Lindsay. D.S.O.

CASUALTIES

Date.	Regt. No.	Rank.	Name.	Remarks.
28.9.15	2635	Private	Carnegie, G.	Wounded.
	2529	Private	Dow, D.	Wounded.
	2056	Private	M'Kenzie, F.W.	Wounded. Died 8.10.15.
30.9.15	1998	Private	Maloney, James	Wounded.
2.10.15	1617	Private	Scott, D.	Wounded.
3.10.15	966	Sergt.	Petrie, R.	Killed.
4.10.15	1799	Private	Clark, T.	Wounded.
6.10.15	1681	Private	Gourlay, J.	Wounded.
9.10.15	2405	Private	Doig, W.S.	Wounded.
11.10.15	2487	Private	Grieve, J.	Wounded.
	1816	Private	Robertson, J.	Wounded.
12.10.15	2039	Private	Westwater, A.C.	Wounded. Died of wounds.
18.10.15	1541	Cpl.	Maxwell, J.	Killed.

Date	Number	Rank	Name	Status
18.10.15	1985	Private	Haworth, F.	Killed.
	1730	Private	Pattinson, J.	Killed.
	1437	L/Sergt.	Valentine, J.	Wounded.
	2029	Private	Roger, W.	Wounded.
19.10.15	2069	Private	Carnegie, R.Y.	Wounded.
20.10.15	2534	Private	Lumsden, T.	Wounded.
	2486	Private	Morris, J.	Wounded. Died of wounds 20.10.15.
21.10.15	2489	Private	Beveridge, H.	Killed.
	1835	Private	Macfarlane, J.	Killed.
	1727	Private	Brown, A.	Wounded.
	2536	Private	O'Neill, J.A.	Wounded.
	1826	Private	Renton, J.	Wounded.
24.10.15	1995	L/Cpl.	Blease, T.	Wounded.
	2081	Private	Young, W.K.	Wounded.
26.10.15	1704	Private	Ford, C.	Killed.
	2201	Private	Henry, J.	Wounded.
27.10.15	2276	Private	Campbell, G.W.	Wounded.
29.10.15	1496	Private	Clark, D.	Killed.

Date	No.	Rank	Name	Status
29.10.15	1449	Sergt.	Farrell, A.	Wounded.
30.10.15	1758	Private	Baxter, J.	Killed.
31.10.15	1971	Private	Kennedy, J.	Killed.
2.11.15	2010	Private	Millar, D.	Wounded.
3.11.15	1989	Private	Rushworth, G.	Died of wounds.
4.11.15	2075	Private	Whyte, J.L.	Wounded.
5.11.15	2535	Private	Jarvis, T.	Wounded.
12.11.15	1705	Private	Cowan, R.	Killed.
		2nd Lieut.	Herdman, C.W.	Wounded.
	1817	Private	Fotheringham, H.	Wounded.
	1751	Private	Harris, W.H.	Wounded.
	1921	Private	Wilson, R.	Wounded.
16.11.15	1621	Private	Fyffe, T.W.	Wounded.
	2216	Private	Gordon, W.	Wounded.
	2204	Private	Pearson, W.	Wounded.
26.11.15	1811	Private	Robertson, R.W.	Wounded.
28.11.15	2043	L/Cpl.	Fairweather, T.	Killed.
	2048	L/Cpl.	Howie, W.	Killed.

Date	Number	Rank	Name	Remarks
28.11.15	1901	Private	Hood, J.T.	Wounded.
	1735	Private	Mitchell, R.R.	Wounded.
	2458	Private	Wilson, J.M.	Wounded.
	2089	Private	Roger, J.M.	Died.
29.11.15	1595	Cpl.	Bowie, R.	Wounded.
	2412	Private	Adamson, D.	Wounded.
	1685	Private	Hamilton, T.	Wounded.
	1930	Private	M'Kechnie, W.	Wounded.
	1563	Private	Millar, T.	Wounded.
	2456	Private	Potter, A.	Wounded.
	2455	Private	Rough, J.	Wounded.
	2337	Private	Wright, C.	Wounded.
	1684	S.S. Cpl.	Pearson, W.	Missing (prisoner). Died at Sivas, 25.5.16.
30.11.15	1886	Private	M'Gregor, R.	Died at Sivas, 25.5.16.
	2083	Private	Moffat, T.	Died at Sivas, 25.5.16.
	2360	Private	Halley, J.	Wounded.
	1581	Cpl.	Peter, A.	Wounded. Died 5.12.15.
1.12.15	2440	Private	Stewart, J.	Wounded. Died of wounds 3.12.15.

2.12.15	1987	R.Q.M.S.	Colclough, W.T.	Wounded.
8.12.15	2209	Private	Batchelor, A.	Wounded.
10.12.15	2021	Private	Galloway, J.	Wounded.
12.12.15	1618	Private	Paton, D.S.	Wounded.
15.12.15	2155	Private	Finlayson, P.	Wounded. Died of wounds 16.12.15.
19.12.15	2057	A/R.Q.M.S.	Craig, J.	Died of wounds.
6.11.15	2186	Private	M'Laren, A.	Died of disease.
8.11.15	2024	Private	Cairns, R.D.	Died of disease.
18.11.15	2129	Private	Harley, A.B.	Died of disease.
15.12.15	2059	S.S.M.	Bradfield, T.	Died of disease.
27.5.16	2026	Private	Hendry, J.M.	Died of disease.
27.11.16	2583	Tptr.	Shearer, W.	Died of disease.
19.4.17	345413	Private	Robertson, R.	Wounded. Mansura Ridge.
	345542	Private	Wilson, H.J.R.	Wounded. Mansura Ridge.
14.5.17	345122	Private	Yule, G.	Wounded.
16.5.17	345060	Saddler	Brown, J.	Wounded and at duty.
25.5.17	345945	L/Sgt.	Bannigan, P.	Killed. Dumb-bell Hill.
	345555	Private	Floyd, J.	Wounded. Dumb-bell Hill.

Date	Number	Rank	Name	Casualty
25.5.17	346003	Private	Wiseman, W.	Wounded. Dumb-bell Hill.
26.5.17	345561	Private	Calder, J.	Wounded and at duty. Dumb-bell Hill.
	340020	Private	M'Donell, D.	Wounded. Dumb-bell Hill.
	340016	Private	Milne, J.W.	Wounded and at duty. Dumb-bell Hill.
31.5.17	345402	Private	Aitkenhead, M.	Wounded and at duty. Dumb-bell Hill.
12.6.17	345934	Private	Davidson, R.	Wounded. Dumb-bell Hill.
17.6.17	345549	Private	Keith, H.	Wounded.
30.8.17	...	2nd Lieut.	Crawford, W.S. (Lanark Yeomanry)	Wounded.
	345180	L/Cpl.	Blease, T.	Wounded.
	345703	Private	Davidson, A.	Wounded and at duty.
	345758	Private	Edwards, J.	Wounded.
	345497	Private	Potter, S.	Wounded and at duty.
1.11.17	345461	L/Cpl.	Harley, R.	Killed.
	345190	Private	Lister, L.	Missing (prisoner).
3.11.17	345073	Cpl.	Dougal, J.F.	Missing (prisoner).
	9276	Private	Bell, A.	Missing (prisoner).
	17468	Private	Brady, J.	Missing (prisoner).
4.11.17	...	2nd Lieut.	Inglis, T.H. (att. Glo'ster Yeomanry).	Wounded.

Date	Number	Rank	Name	Remarks
4.11.17	...	2nd Lieut.	M'Lean, J.	Wounded.
	345335	L/Lieut.	Wyles, A.	Wounded.
	340021	Private	Adams, W.	Wounded.
	345207	Private	Dow, R.	Wounded.
	S/8885	Private	Kirk, G.B.	Wounded.
6.11.17		Major	Osborne, G.E.B.	Killed. Sheria.
		2nd Lieut.	Kinniburgh, J.D.	Killed. Sheria.
		2nd Lieut.	Thomson, E.A.	Killed. Sheria.
	345172	Sergt.	Spence, A.	Killed. Sheria.
	345951	Sergt.	Sharp, J.	Killed. Sheria.
	345633	Cpl.	Dow, J.	Killed. Sheria.
	345161	Cpl.	Ovenstone, P.	Killed. Sheria.
	345264	Cpl.	Rattray, J.M.	Killed. Sheria.
	345627	L/Cpl.	Adamson, H.	Killed. Sheria.
	345953	L/Cpl.	Baxter, R.	Killed. Sheria.
	13133	L/Cpl.	M'Donald, G.	Killed. Sheria.
	345289	L/Cpl.	Prain, G.	Killed. Sheria.
	20382	Private	Anderson, J.	Killed. Sheria.

6.11.17	2819	Private	Aston, T.	Killed. Sheria.
	345332	Private	Braid, D.	Killed. Sheria.
	340004	Private	Combe, W.	Killed. Sheria.
	16294	Private	Dalgleish, W.	Killed. Sheria.
	345545	Private	Downie, H.	Killed. Sheria.
	345605	Private	Fyfe, T.	Killed. Sheria.
	21841	Private	Gault, J.	Killed. Sheria.
	345962	Private	Geddes, C.	Killed. Sheria.
	20390	Private	Hendrie, J.	Killed. Sheria.
	8913	Private	Hoban, P.	Killed. Sheria.
	345301	Private	Howie, G.	Killed. Sheria.
	8224	Private	Hynd, H.	Killed. Sheria.
	345247	Private	Johnstone, J.R.	Killed. Sheria.
	345609	Private	Kemp, W.	Killed. Sheria.
	345717	Private	King, L.	Killed. Sheria.
	345358	Private	Lawrence, A.H.	Killed. Sheria.
	9916	Private	M'Donald, D.	Killed. Sheria.
	340018	Private	M'Millan, D.	Killed. Sheria.

Date	Number	Rank	Name	Note
6.11.17	345679	Private	Milne, J.	Killed. Sheria.
	345871	Private	Milne, J.	Killed. Sheria.
	340016	Private	Milne, J.W.	Killed. Sheria.
	16758	Private	Mudie, F.	Killed. Sheria.
	345350	Private	Muir, J.K.	Killed. Sheria.
	20362	Private	Mutch, C.	Killed. Sheria.
	345115	Private	Nicoll, J.	Killed. Sheria.
	345769	Private	Norman, J.	Killed. Sheria.
	345394	Private	Pake, J.	Killed. Sheria.
	16204	Private	Peattie, D.	Killed. Sheria.
	345598	Private	Ritchie, J.	Killed. Sheria.
	345239	Private	Rodger, W.	Killed. Sheria.
	21819	Private	Ross, D.	Killed. Sheria.
	345735	Private	Scott, R.	Killed. Sheria.
	20889	Private	Staff, J.	Killed. Sheria.
	345861	Private	Stewart, A.	Killed. Sheria.
	345622	Private	Symon, A.	Killed. Sheria.
	345444	Private	Watson, N.	Killed. Sheria.

Date	Number	Rank	Name	Remarks
6.11.17	345325	Private	Wilson, D.	Killed. Sheria.
	19663	Private	Woodward, J.	Killed. Sheria.
		Lt.-Col.	Gilmour, J.	Wounded. Sheria.
		Captain	Campbell, Bart., Sir W.A.A.	Wounded. Sheria.
		Captain	Cummins, W.W.	Wounded. Sheria.
		2nd Lieut.	M'Carrick, F.	Wounded. Sheria.
		2nd Lieut.	Martin, J.M.	Wounded. Sheria.
	345426	Sergt.	Ballantyne, R.	Wounded. Sheria.
	345128	Sergt.	Ballantyne, J.	Wounded. Sheria.
	345416	Sergt.	Collier, W.	Wounded. Sheria.
	345098	Sergt.	Goodall, J.	Wounded. Sheria.
	345947	Sergt.	M'Gregor, H.	Wounded. Sheria.
	345334	Sergt.	Saunders, A.M.	Died of wounds 18.11.17. Sheria.
	345164	Sergt.	Taylor, D.	Died of wounds 11.11.17. Sheria.
	345251	Cpl.	Chalmers, G.C.	Died of wounds 8.11.17. Sheria.
	345097	Cpl.	Farmer, D.	Wounded. Sheria.
	345950	Cpl.	Hedley, W.	Wounded. Sheria.
	345138	Cpl.	Hood, J.T.	Wounded. Sheria.

6.11.17	345234	Cpl.	Moir, A.	Wounded. Sheria.
	345341	Cpl.	Patterson, T.	Wounded. Sheria.
	345398	Cpl.	Rollo, D.	Wounded. Sheria.
	345196	Cpl.	Stewart, G.	Wounded. Sheria.
	345030	Cpl.	Whyte, J.	Wounded. Sheria.
	345223	Cpl.	Wright, R.H.	Wounded. Sheria.
	345225	L/Cpl.	Black, D.	Wounded. Sheria.
	345917	L/Cpl.	Cairncross, H.	Wounded. Sheria.
	340001	L/Cpl.	Dick, J.	Wounded. Sheria.
	345816	L/Cpl.	Doig, R.	Wounded. Sheria.
	345054	L/Cpl.	Fleming, A.	Wounded. Sheria.
	345174	L/Cpl.	Flynn, W.	Died of wounds. Sheria.
	345244	L/Cpl.	Hamilton, W.	Wounded. Sheria.
	345780	L/Cpl.	Holmes, R.	Wounded. Sheria.
	345844	L/Cpl.	Honeyman, J.	Wounded. Sheria.
	345074	L/Cpl.	Leitch, J.J.	Wounded. Sheria.
	345015	L/Cpl.	Lister, H.	Wounded. Sheria.
	345188	L/Cpl.	Ogg, J.	Wounded. Sheria.

6.11.17	345471	L/Cpl.	Stephen, E.	Wounded. Sheria.
	18945	L/Cpl.	Ward, C.	Wounded. Sheria.
	345395	L/Cpl.	Wright, W.	Wounded. Sheria.
	15545	L/Cpl.	Younger, J.	Wounded. Sheria.
	345918	Private	Alexander, P.	Wounded. Sheria.
	15794	Private	Allan, J.	Wounded. Sheria.
	340002	Private	Angus, T.	Wounded. Sheria.
	345576	Private	Armstrong, W.	Died of wounds 29.11.8. Sheria.
	345834	Private	Bagridge, H.	Wounded. Sheria.
	345998	Private	Barlow, W.R.	Wounded. Sheria.
	345579	Private	Beaton, J.	Wounded. Sheria.
	345496	Private	Birrell, H.	Wounded. Sheria.
	345577	Private	Bisset, A.	Wounded. Sheria.
	345405	Private	Black, G.	Wounded. Sheria.
	345695	Private	Black, J.	Wounded. Sheria.
	345478	Private	Blyth, J.	Wounded. Sheria.
	345747	Private	Boyle, J.	Wounded. Sheria.
	346000	Private	Bradshaw, A.	Wounded. Sheria.

6.11.17	345890	Bremner, F.	Private	Wounded. Sheria.
	345561	Calder, J.	Private	Wounded. Sheria.
	345312	Calderhead, J.	Private	Wounded. Sheria.
	345268	Campbell, G.W.	Private	Wounded. Sheria.
	345635	Campbell, J.	Private	Wounded. Sheria.
	18725	Cant, A.	Private	Wounded. Sheria.
	20876	Chalmers, J.	Private	Wounded. Sheria.
	345878	Chalmers, W.	Private	Wounded. Sheria.
	241313	Clarkson, J.R.	Private	Wounded. Sheria.
	340006	Colthart, T.	Private	Wounded. Sheria.
	345678	Conning, J.	Private	Wounded. Sheria.
	22141	Cooper, W.	Private	Wounded. Sheria.
	345092	Coupar, D.L.	Private	Wounded. Sheria.
	345869	Craig, G.	Private	Wounded. Sheria.
	11824	Craig, J.	Private	Wounded. Sheria.
	345152	Crichton, W.	Private	Wounded. Sheria.
	345854	Crighton, A.	Private	Wounded. Sheria.
	345591	Cumming, J.	Private	Wounded. Sheria.

Date	Number	Name	Rank	Notes
6.11.17	345275	Denholm, C.	Private	Wounded. Sheria.
	345648	Devlin, C.	Private	Wounded. Sheria.
	43091	Donaldson, D.	Private	Wounded. Sheria.
	18718	Drysdale, A.	Private	Wounded. Sheria.
	345704	Duffin, J.	Private	Died of wounds 23.11.17. Sheria.
	345238	Duncan, G.	Private	Wounded. Sheria.
	345154	Dunn, W.	Private	Wounded. Sheria.
	20381	Edwards, D.	Private	Died of wounds 8.11.17. Sheria.
	21824	Ellison, S.	Private	Wounded. Sheria.
	345567	Emerson, F.	Private	Wounded. Sheria.
	340013	Ewart, J.	Private	Wounded. Sheria.
	345649	Ferguson, H.	Private	Wounded. Sheria.
	20878	Findlay, W.	Private	Wounded. Sheria.
	345963	Finlayson, A.C.	Private	Wounded. Sheria.
	345568	Forsyth, J.B.	Private	Wounded. Sheria.
	345434	Gibb, D.	Private	Wounded. Sheria.
	4570	Gordon, W.	Private	Wounded. Sheria.
	345507	Grant, A.	Private	Wounded. Sheria.

Date	Number	Rank	Name	Status
6.11.17	345534	Private	Gray, J.	Wounded. Sheria.
	20378	Private	Gunn, A.	Wounded. Sheria.
	22331	Private	Gunn, D.	Wounded. Sheria.
	345713	Private	Guyan, D.	Died of wounds 11.11.17. Sheria.
	345654	Private	Helmsley, P.	Wounded. Sheria.
	345898	Private	Henderson, W.	Wounded. Sheria.
	345495	Private	Henderson, J.	Wounded. Sheria.
	345282	Private	Henry, T.B.	Wounded. Sheria.
	241311	Private	Herbertson, J.	Wounded. Sheria.
	10507	Private	Herd, D.	Wounded. Sheria.
	10507	Private	Hirst, R.	Wounded. Sheria.
	345510	Private	Hunter, R.	Wounded. Sheria.
	345763	Private	King, B.	Died of wounds 6.1.18. Sheria.
	345990	Private	Laing, J.	Wounded. Sheria.
	345926	Private	Langston, H.	Wounded. Sheria.
	345965	Private	Lawson, A.M.	Wounded. Sheria.
	345611	Private	Linn, J.	Wounded. Sheria.
	345612	Private	Livingstone, G.	Wounded. Sheria.

6.11.17	345901	Private	Lockhart, A.	Wounded. Sheria.
	3752	Private	Lyall, P.	Died of wounds 7.11.17. Sheria.
	345783	Private	M'Aree, H.	Wounded. Sheria.
	345385	Private	M'Call, J.	Wounded. Sheria.
	20379	Private	M'Carthey, J.	Wounded. Sheria.
	345483	Private	M'Cartney, W.H.	Wounded. Sheria.
	345266	Private	M'Donald, A.	Wounded. Sheria.
	340020	Private	M'Donald, D.	Wounded. Sheria.
	345269	Private	M'Donald, F.	Died of wounds 8.11.17. Sheria.
	345975	Private	M'Donald, J.	Wounded. Sheria.
	345354	Private	M'Ewan, T.	Died of wounds 8.11.17. Sheria.
	345628	Private	M'Fadden, H.	Wounded. Sheria.
	345822	Private	M'Goldrick, F.	Wounded. Sheria.
	345460	Private	M'Graw, D.	Wounded. Sheria.
	345724	Private	M'Inroy, D.	Wounded. Sheria.
	345401	Private	M'Kechnie, W.	Wounded. Sheria.
	345587	Private	M'Laggan, J.	Wounded. Sheria.
	345611	Private	M'Millan, A.	Wounded. Sheria.

Date	Number	Name	Rank	Status
6.11.17	345680	M'Millan, J.	Private	Died of wounds 6.11.17. Sheria.
	345967	M'Rae, M.	Private	Wounded. Sheria.
	345971	Marshall, J.	Private	Wounded. Sheria.
	16505	Martin, J.	Private	Wounded. Sheria.
	345659	Martin, W.	Private	Wounded. Sheria.
	345406	Mathew, J.	Private	Wounded. Sheria.
	345728	Meekison, C.	Private	Wounded. Sheria.
	345824	Meldrum, A.	Private	Wounded. Sheria.
	20394	Mercer, H.	Private	Died of wounds 8.11.17. Sheria.
	345439	Moir, J.	Private	Wounded. Sheria.
	345260	Moonie, J.W.	Private	Wounded. Sheria.
	345566	Morgan, S.	Private	Wounded. Sheria.
	345658	Mudie, W.	Private	Wounded. Sheria.
	345910	Murray, T.	Private	Wounded. Sheria.
	345482	Penman, A.	Private	Wounded. Sheria.
	345290	Pennycook, J.M.	Private	Wounded. Sheria.
	16033	Petrie, D.	Private	Wounded. Sheria.
	345597	Prain, S.	Private	Wounded. Sheria.

6.11.17	345929	Private	Purvis, D.	Wounded. Sheria.
	345976	Private	Ramsay, W.	Wounded. Sheria.
	345977	Private	Reid, M.	Wounded. Sheria.
	20875	Private	Reid, R.	Wounded. Sheria.
	345573	Private	Rennie, C.	Wounded. Sheria.
	345982	Private	Robertson, A.	Wounded. Sheria.
	345556	Private	Robertson, J.	Wounded. Sheria.
	345392	Private	Robertson, W.	Died of wounds 12.11.17. Sheria.
	346010	Private	Roy, A.	Died of wounds 12.11.17. Sheria.
	345575	Private	Scott, A.	Died of wounds 12.11.17. Sheria.
	345486	Private	Seath, J.	Died of wounds 12.11.17. Sheria.
	18720	Private	Shepherd, D.	Died of wounds 12.11.17. Sheria.
	345249	Private	Simpson, A.	Died of wounds 12.11.17. Sheria.
	345995	Private	Simpson, J.	Died of wounds 12.11.17. Sheria.
	345808	Private	Smith, R.	Died of wounds 12.11.17. Sheria.
	345333	Private	Smith, W.	Died of wounds 12.11.17. Sheria.
	20865	Private	Smith, W.A.	Died of wounds 12.11.17. Sheria.
	340012	Private	Soutar, W.	Died of wounds 12.11.17. Sheria.

6.11.17	345741	Private	Spence, G.	Died of wounds 12.11.17. Sheria.
	346011	Private	Stewart, C.	Died of wounds 12.11.17. Sheria.
	345585	Private	Storey, C.	Died of wounds 12.11.17. Sheria.
	345068	Private	Storrar, M.	Died of wounds 12.11.17. Sheria.
	345775	Private	Stronner, J.	Died of wounds 12.11.17. Sheria.
	345529	Private	Stuart, J.	Died of wounds 12.11.17. Sheria.
	345415	Private	Thomson, H.	Died of wounds 12.11.17. Sheria.
	345862	Private	Turner, G.	Died of wounds 12.11.17. Sheria.
	19848	Private	Twist, T.	Died of wounds 12.11.17. Sheria.
	345599	Private	Urquhart, J.	Died of wounds 12.11.17. Sheria.
	345468	Private	Veale, L.	Wounded. Sheria.
	340022	Private	Walker, G.	Wounded. Sheria.
	345687	Private	Waterson, T.	Wounded. Sheria.
	15462	Private	Weston, A.	Wounded. Sheria.
	345784	Private	Whyte, R.	Wounded. Sheria.
	345506	Private	Wilson, J.	Wounded. Sheria.
	345317	Private	Wilson, J.	Wounded. Sheria.
	20895	Private	Williamson, T.	Wounded. Sheria.

Date	Number	Rank	Name	Remarks
6.11.17	20376	Private	Woodward, R.A.	Wounded. Sheria.
	345946	Captain	Brown, W.D.	Wounded and at duty. Sheria.
		Sergt.	Mackie, A.	Wounded and at duty. Sheria.
	345087	L/Cpl.	Reid, I.	Wounded and at duty. Sheria.
	345020	L/Cpl.	Robertson, K.	Wounded and at duty. Sheria.
	345615	Private	M'Leod, N.	Wounded and at duty. Sheria.
	345666	Private	Petrie, M.	Wounded and at duty. Sheria.
	345075	Private	Rodger, D.	Wounded and at duty. Sheria.
	345383	Private	Ross, G.R.	Wounded and at duty. Sheria.
	345317	Private	Wilson, J.	Wounded and at duty. Sheria.
30.11.17	345002	C.Q.M.S	Morrison, D.	Wounded. Wadi Selman.
	345051	Sergt.	Watson, J.	Wounded. Wadi Selman.
	345430	L/Sergt.	M'Neil, R.	Wounded. Wadi Selman.
	345638	Private	Benson, H.	Wounded. Wadi Selman.
	345899	Private	Higginbottom, R.	Wounded. Wadi Selman.
	18845	Private	Huckerby, W.	Wounded. Wadi Selman.
	293275	Private	Smith, E.J.	Wounded. Wadi Selman.
	13401	Private	Paxton, R.	Wounded and at duty. Selman.

Date	Number	Rank	Name	Remarks
1.12.17		2nd Lieut.	Greenlees, G.D.	Killed. "1750."
	345352	Private	Dickson, D.G.	Killed. "1750."
	345857	Private	Plant, H.	Wounded and at duty. "1750."
3.12.17	345712	Private	Gray, W.	Missing (prisoner).
10.12.17	345814	Private	Connaghan, M.	Wounded.
27.12.17		2nd Lieut.	Forrest, P.T.A.	Killed. Zeitun.
		2nd Lieut.	Armstrong, W.W.	Killed. Zeitun.
	21840	Private	Anderson, J.	Killed. Zeitun.
	9388	Private	Brand, J.	Killed. Zeitun.
	345698	Private	Brookland, F.	Killed. Zeitun.
	21826	Private	Goodfellow, J.	Killed. Zeitun.
	345969	Private	Jack, A.	Killed. Zeitun.
	346009	Private	Patterson, J.C.	Killed. Zeitun.
	345524	Private	Young, P.	Killed. Zeitun.
		Captain	Brown, W.D.	Died of wounds 27.12.17. Zeitun.
	345214	Sergt.	Menzies, J.B.	Wounded. Zeitun.
	5756	L/Sergt.	Grant, D.	Wounded. Zeitun.
	345422	Cpl.	Bisset, D.	Wounded. Zeitun.

27.12.17	345080	L/Cpl.	Mackay, R.B.	Wounded. Zeitun.
	345565	L/Cpl.	M'Whirter, D.	Wounded. Zeitun.
	2491	L/Cpl.	Silvester, W.	Wounded. Zeitun.
	21715	L/Cpl.	Williams, J.P.	Died of wounds 28.12.17. Zeitun.
	345425	Private	Braid, T.	Died of wounds 29.12.17. Zeitun.
	26887	Private	Clunie, R.	Died of wounds 29.12.17. Zeitun.
	345647	Private	Dunk, P.	Wounded. Zeitun.
	345838	Private	Ferguson, W.	Wounded. Zeitun.
	7194	Private	Freal, S.	Died of wounds 2.1.18. Zeitun.
	345842	Private	Hickman, C.	Died of wounds. Zeitun.
	345384	Private	Knox, R.	Wounded. Zeitun.
	18716	Private	M'Intosh, E.	Wounded. Zeitun.
	345586	Private	M'Intyre, W.	Died of wounds 11.4.18. Zeitun.
	345662	Private	M'Kendrick, A.	Wounded. Zeitun.
	345522	Private	M'Pherson, M.	Wounded. Zeitun.
	20368	Private	Paton, F.	Wounded. Zeitun.
	268743	Private	Patterson, A.	Wounded. Zeitun.
	240198	Private	Smith, R.M.	Wounded. Zeitun.

Date	Number	Rank	Name	Status
27.12.17	345337	Private	Tocher, A.	Wounded. Zeitun.
	22243	Private	Van Riel, H.F.	Wounded. Zeitun.
	345273	Sergt.	Halley, R.	Wounded and at duty. Zeitun.
28.12.17		Lieut.	Johnstone, W.J.	Killed. Beitania.
		2nd Lieut.	Paisley, G. W.	Killed (with A. & L. Yeo.). Beitania.
	345200	Sergt.	Syme, W.	Killed. Beitania.
	345009	L/Sergt.	Oliver, R.	Killed. Beitania.
	345270	L/Cpl.	Dickson, W.	Killed. Beitania.
	345751	Private	Byrne, T.	Killed. Beitania.
	345815	Private	Crighton, C.	Killed. Beitania.
	241316	Private	M'Kinnon, A.	Killed. Beitania.
	345311	Private	Reid, J.	Killed. Beitania.
	18698	Private	Ross, D.	Killed. Beitania.
		Captain	Duncan, P.F.	Wounded. Beitania.
		2nd Lieut.	Cummings, D.	Wounded. Beitania.
		2nd Lieut.	Haggart, J.	Died of wounds 3.1.18. Beitania.
		2nd Lieut.	Robson, P.L.	Wounded. Beitania.
	345053	Sergt.	Boath, W.	Wounded. Beitania.

28.12.17	345273	Sergt.	Halley, R.	Wounded. Beitania.
	345165	Sergt.	Hogg, R.M.	Wounded. Beitania.
	345404	L/Cpl.	Kilpatrick, W.	Died of wounds 29.12.17. Beitania.
	18684	L/Cpl.	Rankine, T.	Wounded. Beitania.
	345511	L/Cpl.	Rodgerson, D.	Wounded. Beitania.
	345578	Private	Beveridge, R.	Wounded. Beitania.
	345786	Private	Blyth, G.	Wounded. Beitania.
	345194	Private	Brady, H.	Wounded. Beitania.
	203197	Private	Buntain, J.	Wounded. Beitania.
	16034	Private	Christie, G.D.	Wounded. Beitania.
	3688	Private	Cowan, A.	Wounded. Beitania.
	14709	Private	Davidson, A.	Died of wounds 30.12.17. Beitania.
	345459	Private	Davidson, H.	Wounded. Beitania.
	340025	Private	Easson, W.	Wounded. Beitania.
	200549	Private	Flynn, W.	Wounded. Beitania.
	345236	Private	Henderson, W.	Wounded. Beitania.
	22027	Private	Inglis, J.	Wounded. Beitania.
	345252	Private	Johnstone, G.A.	Wounded. Beitania.

28.12.17	240369	M'Callum, W.	Private	Wounded. Beitania.
	13009	M'Ginley, R.	Private	Wounded. Beitania.
	345613	M'Kay, P.	Private	Wounded. Beitania.
	345927	M'Killop, P.	Private	Wounded. Beitania.
	17064	Minchella, P.	Private	Wounded. Beitania.
	14227	Mitchell, A.	Private	Wounded. Beitania.
	21828	Morrison, G.	Private	Wounded. Beitania.
	8742	Munro, S.	Private	Wounded. Beitania.
	345682	Potter, L.	Private	Wounded. Beitania.
	345512	Robertson, W.P.	Private	Wounded. Beitania.
	20390	Roper, J.	Private	Wounded. Beitania.
	18978	Small, A.	Private	Wounded. Beitania.
	12500	Smith, J.	Private	Wounded. Beitania.
	345984	Smith, W.	Private	Wounded. Beitania.
	345209	Spence, T.	Private	Wounded. Beitania.
	21820	Taylor, T.	Private	Died of wounds 29.12.17. Beitania.
	40617	Watterson, J.	Private	Wounded. Beitania.
	345745	Wheeler, J.	Private	Wounded. Beitania.

28.12.17	345518	Private	Williamson, J.A.	Wounded. Beitania.
	345464	Private	Young, W.D.	Wounded. Beitania.
	345575	Private	Mitchell, W.	Wounded. Beitania.
	345130	Private	Young, H.	Wounded. Beitania.
14.4.17	12701	L/Cpl.	Drinnan, G.	Drowned *ex* H.M.T., *Arcadian*.
	18724	Private	Findlater, J.	Drowned *ex* H.M.T., *Arcadian*.
	18703	Private	Wann, R.	Drowned *ex* H.M.T., *Arcadian*.
	18697	Private	Williams, A.	Drowned *ex* H.M.T., *Arcadian*.
4.5.17	20373	Private	Brown, W.J.	Drowned *ex* H.M.T., *Transylvania*.
	20880	Private	Chisholm, A.	Drowned *ex* H.M.T., *Transylvania*.
	20386	Private	Denholm, J.	Drowned *ex* H.M.T., *Transylvania*.
	20380	Private	Houston, W.	Drowned *ex* H.M.T., *Transylvania*.
	20393	Private	Jones, W.L.	Drowned *ex* H.M.T., *Transylvania*.
	20366	Private	Shenken, P.	Drowned *ex* H.M.T., *Transylvania*.
	20890	Private	Smith, J.	Drowned *ex* H.M.T., *Transylvania*.
	20893	Private	Stewart, C.	Drowned *ex* H.M.T., *Transylvania*.
	20867	Private	Thompson, J.	Drowned *ex* H.M.T., *Transylvania*.
30.12.17	202466	L/Cpl.	Stenhouse, J.	Drowned *ex* H.M.T., *Aragon*.

Date	Number	Rank	Name	Remarks
30.12.17	266648	Private	Small, R.	Drowned *ex* H.M.T., *Aragon.*
	292849	Private	Wood, E.	Drowned *ex* H.M.T., *Aragon.*
20.3.17	345774	Private	Reid, J.	Died.
14.4.17	345736	Private	Shepherd, J.	Died.
12.11.17	345411	Private	Melville, J.	Died.
4.12.17	345494	Private	Ewing, A.	Died.
10.3.18	20121	Private	Keith, J.	Wounded and at duty.
22.3.18	300030	Sergt.	Livingstone R.A.M.C. (attached).	Wounded and at duty.
26.3.18	345445	Private	Ferguson, R.	Killed.
	345140	Private	Carrie, A.F.	Wounded.
	345852	Private	M'Guffog, A.	Wounded.
	345130	Private	Young, H.	Wounded.
	345104	Cpl.	Conacher, J.	Wounded and at duty.
2.4.18	345550	Private	Fagan, H.	Wounded and at duty.
6.4.18		Captain	Down, N.C.S.	Wounded.
	345021	C.Q.M.S.	Blyth, D.	Wounded and at duty.
	345648	Private	Devlin, C.	Wounded and at duty.
	345177	Private	Ramsay, J.	Wounded and at duty.

Date	Number	Rank	Name	Remarks
24.7.18	345636	Cpl.	Bruce, W.	Wounded.
	345395	L/Cpl.	Wright, W.	Wounded.
	22156	Private	Bingham, J.	Wounded.
	345699	Private	Rodger, A.	Wounded.
	345884	Private	Young, J.	Wounded.
	345157	Sergt.	Paris, J.	Wounded and at duty.
	9090	Cpl.	Halkett, J.	Wounded and at duty.
	345646	Private	Clark, C.	Wounded and at duty.
	20881	Private	Florence, R.	Wounded and at duty.
	15200	Private	Fraser, D.	Wounded and at duty.
	22177	Private	Heddleston, J.	Wounded and at duty.
	345655	Private	Herd, J.	Wounded and at duty.
	345669	Private	Samson, A.	Wounded and at duty.
25.7.18	18192	Private	Findlay, W.	Wounded. Died of wounds 24.9.18.
31.7.18	203396	Private	Braynion, W.	Wounded.
4.8.18		2nd Lieut.	Fraser, H.L.	Wounded.
	345277	Sergt.	Campbell, W.	Wounded.
	345447	Private	Allen, J.	Wounded.

4.8.18	345559	Private	Donald, J.	Wounded.
	345628	Private	M'Fadden, H.	Wounded.
	203190	Private	Nimmo, R.	Wounded.
	21837	Private	Taylor, J.	Wounded.
	345438	Private	Wilson, A.	Wounded.
	345237	Private	Cameron, D.	Wounded and at duty.
	345968	Private	Mann, G.	Wounded and at duty.
5.8.18	346042	Private	Morgan, G.	Wounded and at duty.
	20888	Private	Kane, J.	Wounded and at duty.
7.8.18	11944	Private	Walker, D.	Killed.
	315095	Sergt.	M'Niven, A., R.A.M.C. (attached).	Wounded.
	11463	Private	Armour, J.	Wounded.
	16360	Private	Berry, C.	Wounded.
	345500	Private	Hunter, J.	Wounded.
	345252	Private	Johnston, G.A.	Wounded.
	345824	Private	Meldrum, A.	Wounded.
	22031	Private	Todd, M.	Wounded.
8.8.18	20879	L/Cpl.	Strachan, J.	Killed.

Date	Number	Rank	Name	Status
8.8.18	268173	Private	Aitken, J.	Killed.
	15200	Private	Fraser, D.	Killed.
	22157	Private	Wilson, A.	Killed.
	13697	Cpl.	Hardinge, A.	Wounded.
	345530	Cpl.	Mackie, C.B.	Wounded.
	345466	Private	Brady, J.	Wounded.
	20881	Private	Florence, R.	Wounded.
	345607	Private	Greenhill, R.	Wounded.
	22162	Private	Kilgour, W.	Wounded.
	8885	Private	Kirk, G.	Wounded.
	345790	Private	M'Coubray, J.	Wounded.
	266686	Private	M'Rae, R.	Wounded.
	2592	Private	Paul, J. (attached T.M.B.)	Wounded.
	345472	Private	Wilson, J.	Wounded.
9.8.18	16403	Private	Wilson, G. (attached T.M.B.)	Killed.
	20677	Private	Edmiston, J.	Wounded.
	345682	Private	Potter, L.	Wounded.
	22183	Private	Simpson, J.	Wounded.

Date	Number	Rank	Name	Remarks
9.8.18	346013	Private	Wilson, A.	Wounded.
	345575	Private	Scott, A.	Wounded and at duty.
	345435	Private	White, H. (229th Brigade H.Q.).	Wounded and at duty.
10.8.18	6153	Private	Frizzell, R.	Killed.
	345318	L/Cpl.	Nicol, J.	Wounded.
	18683	Private	Connelly, J.	Wounded.
	345754	Private	Crighton, A.	Wounded.
	345647	Private	Dunk, P.	Wounded.
	5036	Private	Osborne, W.	Wounded.
	203198	Private	Stewart, A.	Wounded and at duty.
13.8.18	345413	Private	Robertson, R.	Wounded and at duty.
25.8.18	20376	Private	Woodward, R.A.	Wounded. Died of wounds 27.8.18.
	9344	Private	Murray, W.	Wounded and at duty.
2.9.18		Captain	Stewart, R.W.	Killed. Moislains.
		Captain	Nairn, I.C., M.C.	Killed. Moislains.
		2nd Lieut.	Darney, C.E.	Killed. Moislains.
	345028	Sergt.	M'Kenzie, W.	Killed. Moislains.
	345950	L/Sergt.	Hedley, W.	Killed. Moislains.

2.9.18	345988	L/Sergt.	Walton, F.	Killed. Moislains.
	345390	Cpl.	Keith, W.	Killed. Moislains.
	345105	L/Cpl.	Boyd, W.	Killed. Moislains.
	345355	L/Cpl.	Husband, W.	Killed. Moislains.
	345553	Private	Anderson, R.	Killed. Moislains.
	345638	Private	Benson, H.	Killed. Moislains.
	345577	Private	Bissett, A.	Killed. Moislains.
	22250	Private	Blair, D.	Killed. Moislains.
	345561	Private	Calder, J.	Killed. Moislains.
	22141	Private	Cooper, W.A.	Killed. Moislains.
	16513	Private	Duncan, T.	Killed. Moislains.
	203208	Private	Elder, G.	Killed. Moislains.
	201336	Private	Ferguson, J.	Killed. Moislains.
	345760	Private	Hamilton, R.	Killed. Moislains.
	22177	Private	Heddleston, J.	Killed. Moislains.
	345842	Private	Hickman, C.	Killed. Moislains.
	203207	Private	Irwin, J.	Killed. Moislains.
	20121	Private	Keith, J.	Killed. Moislains.

2.9.18	201992	Private	Lambie, H.	Killed. Moislains.
	13703	Private	M'Ilwain, A.	Killed. Moislains.
	345587	Private	M'Laggan, J.	Killed. Moislains.
	345726	Private	M'Lean, T.	Killed. Moislains.
	345968	Private	Mann, G.	Killed. Moislains.
	345149	Private	Melville, L. W.	Killed. Moislains.
	345526	Private	Millar, R.	Killed. Moislains.
	345260	Private	Moonie, J. W.	Killed. Moislains.
	9344	Private	Murray, W.	Killed. Moislains.
	203204	Private	Reid, J.	Killed. Moislains.
	29712	Private	Reid, R.	Killed. Moislains.
	345733	Private	Rodger, J.	Killed. Moislains.
	20371	Private	Shanks, A.	Killed. Moislains.
	22831	Private	Smith, R.	Killed. Moislains.
	22180	Private	Sneddon, P.	Killed. Moislains.
	3875	Private	Thomson, J.	Killed. Moislains.
	345866	Private	Wilkie, A.	Killed. Moislains.
		Lt.-Col.	Younger, J.	Wounded. Moislains.

2.9.18

	Rank	Name	Remarks
	Captain	M'Nab, J.B.	Wounded. Moislains.
	Lieut.	Duncan, C.G.	Wounded. Moislains.
	2nd Lieut.	Clydesdale, R.A.	Wounded. Moislains.
	2nd Lieut.	Laing, J.E.	Wounded. Moislains.
	2nd Lieut.	Grant, J.W.	Wounded. Moislains.
	2nd Lieut.	Dawes, J.W.	Wounded. Moislains.
	2nd Lieut.	Van Millingen, D.F.	Wounded. Moislains.
	2nd Lieut.	Craigen, J.W.W.	Wounded. Moislains.
	2nd Lieut.	Dickie, J.A.	Wounded. Moislains.
345001	C.S.M.	Aitken, A.	Wounded. Died of wounds 2.9.18.
345136	Sergt.	Andrews, A.	Wounded. Moislains.
345097	Sergt.	Farmer, D.	Wounded. Moislains.
6069	Sergt.	Green, J.	Wounded. Moislains.
345887	Sergt.	M'Donald, J.	Wounded. Moislains.
3796	Sergt.	M'Laren, P.	Wounded. Died of wounds 3.9.18.
5306	Sergt.	Meiklejohn, T.	Wounded. Moislains.
345941	Sergt.	Mickel, H.W.	Wounded. Moislains.
345886	Sergt.	Spence, J.	Wounded. Died of wounds 7.9.18.

2.9.18	9090	L/Sergt.	Halkett, J.	Wounded. Moislains.
	345920	Cpl.	Airth, C.	Wounded. Moislains.
	3056	Cpl.	Blues, J.	Wounded. Moislains.
	345811	Cpl.	Brown, A.	Wounded. Moislains.
	22194	Cpl.	Cattanach, T.J.	Wounded. Moislains.
	345242	Cpl.	Cheape, J.	Wounded. Moislains.
	18847	Cpl.	Douglas, S.	Wounded. Died of wounds 5.9.18.
	345721	Cpl.	Marnock, W.	Wounded. Moislains.
	5357	Cpl.	M'Dougal, T.	Wounded. Moislains.
	22188	Cpl.	Price, J.	Wounded. Moislains.
	345580	L/Cpl.	Deans, S.	Wounded. Moislains.
	345094	L/Cpl.	Dickie, H. (D.C.M.)	Wounded. Died of wounds 4.9.18.
	14721	L/Cpl.	Duncan, F.	Wounded. Moislains.
	11279	L/Cpl.	Eddie, R.	Wounded. Moislains.
	345342	L/Cpl.	Greig, W.T.	Wounded. Moislains.
	345993	L/Cpl.	Hall, T.D.	Wounded. Moislains.
	20864	L/Cpl.	Jessiman, W.	Wounded. Moislains.
	202135	L/Cpl.	M'Intyre, D.	Wounded. Moislains.

2.9.18	265246	L/Cpl.	Manuel, J.	Wounded. Moislains.
	345969	L/Cpl.	Milton, M.	Wounded. Moislains.
	345670	L/Cpl.	Smith, P.	Wounded. Moislains.
	203198	L/Cpl.	Stewart, A.	Wounded. Moislains.
	345525	L/Cpl.	Wilson, F.	Wounded. Moislains.
	22192	Private	Alexander, G.	Wounded. Moislains.
	345167	Private	Alexander, R.	Wounded. Moislains.
	41422	Private	Allan, W.	Wounded. Moislains.
	345889	Private	Anderson, A.	Wounded. Moislains.
	345639	Private	Anderson, D.	Wounded. Moislains.
	16495	Private	Belford, J.B.	Wounded. Moislains.
	346023	Private	Bibb, H.	Wounded. Moislains.
	22164	Private	Blackwood, G.T.	Wounded. Moislains.
	345371	Private	Blyth, W.	Wounded. Moislains.
	290402	Private	Brown, D.	Wounded. Moislains.
	345955	Private	Buchan, M.	Wounded. Moislains.
	203197	Private	Buntain, J.	Wounded. Moislains.
	241199	Private	Burgess, A.	Wounded. Moislains.

2.9.18	345257	Private	Burnett, H.	Wounded. Moislains.
	20750	Private	Burns, G.	Wounded. Moislains.
	345891	Private	Cameron, J.	Wounded. Moislains.
	345268	Private	Campbell, G.W.	Wounded. Moislains.
	267932	Private	Campbell, T.W.	Wounded. Moislains.
	40460	Private	Carmichael, D.	Wounded. Moislains.
	345940	Private	Cassells, W.	Wounded. Moislains.
	20876	Private	Chalmers, J.	Wounded. Moislains.
	241313	Private	Clarkson, J.R.	Wounded. Moislains.
	290777	Private	Colville, H.	Wounded. Moislains.
	41439	Private	Cooney, B.	Wounded. Moislains.
	345310	Private	Cran, J.	Wounded. Moislains.
	345703	Private	Davidson, A.	Wounded. Moislains.
	20882	Private	Donnett, W.	Wounded. Moislains.
	345207	Private	Dow, R.	Wounded. Moislains.
	202972	Private	Dunipace, W.	Wounded. Died of wounds 6.9.18.
	14723	Private	Eadie, F.	Wounded. Moislains.
	345101	Private	Edwards, G.R.	Wounded. Moislains.

2.9.18	345593	Private	Ewing, A.	Wounded. Moislains.
	345550	Private	Fagan, H.	Wounded. Moislains.
	345215	Private	Fairley, D.	Wounded. Moislains.
	345759	Private	Fleming, W.	Wounded. Moislains.
	346007	Private	Flockhart, D.	Wounded. Moislains.
	345789	Private	Gardiner, R.	Wounded. Moislains.
	345961	Private	Gillan, J.	Wounded. Moislains.
	241346	Private	Gow, W.	Wounded. Moislains.
	345267	Private	Greig, J.G.	Wounded. Moislains.
	345651	Private	Hagan, J.	Wounded. Moislains.
	345569	Private	Haines, L.	Wounded. Moislains.
	346040	Private	Hanlon, G.	Wounded. Moislains.
	345653	Private	Hay, J.	Wounded. Moislains.
	345655	Private	Herd, J.	Wounded. Moislains.
	345143	Private	Hirst, S.	Wounded. Moislains.
	345844	Private	Honeyman, J.	Wounded. Moislains.
	9620	Private	Hunter, W.	Wounded. Moislains.
	290189	Private	Hutchison, W.	Wounded. Moislains.

2.9.18	5308	Private	Inglis, W.	Wounded. Moislains.
	345845	Private	Jamieson, D.	Wounded. Moislains.
	20888	Private	Kane, J.	Wounded. Moislains.
	345657	Private	Lang, J.	Wounded. Moislains.
	345720	Private	Lightfoot, J.	Wounded. Moislains.
	345271	Private	M'Askill, A.	Wounded. Moislains.
	265722	Private	M'Callum, C.	Wounded. Moislains.
	268529	Private	M'Diarmid, D.	Wounded. Moislains.
	345975	Private	M'Donald, J.	Wounded. Moislains.
	340008	Private	M'Donald, T.	Wounded. Moislains.
	22182	Private	M'Dowell, G.	Wounded. Moislains.
	22324	Private	M'Kay, F.	Wounded. Moislains.
	346028	Private	M'Kenzie, A.	Wounded. Moislains.
	22187	Private	M'Kenzie, W.	Wounded. Moislains.
	345552	Private	M'Kenna, J.	Wounded. Moislains.
	345661	Private	M'Millan, J.	Wounded. Moislains.
	22204	Private	Marchant, J.	Wounded. Moislains.
	22198	Private	Mearns, J.	Wounded. Moislains.

2.9.18	266895	Private	Merrylees, A.	Wounded. Moislains.
	340011	Private	Milne, J.S.	Wounded. Moislains.
	345660	Private	Mitchell, D.J.	Wounded. Moislains.
	22142	Private	Mitchell, W.	Wounded. Moislains.
	345554	Private	Montgomery, J.	Wounded. Moislains.
	346008	Private	Morris, W.	Wounded. Moislains.
	345910	Private	Murray, T.	Wounded. Moislains.
	43455	Private	Ness, T.	Wounded. Moislains.
	345119	Private	Niven, R.	Wounded. Died of wounds 6.9.18.
	340027	Private	Norrie, A.	Wounded. Moislains.
	43301	Private	Ogilvie, D.	Wounded. Moislains.
	345276	Private	Page, D.	Wounded. Moislains.
	345619	Private	Petrie, J.	Wounded. Moislains.
	16698	Private	Philip, A.	Wounded. Moislains.
	345682	Private	Potter, L.	Wounded. Moislains.
	41524	Private	Rait, T.	Wounded. Moislains.
	345321	Private	Ramsay, J.	Wounded. Moislains.
	345278	Private	Reid, J.	Wounded. Moislains.

2.9.18	345977	Private	Reid, M.D.	Wounded. Moislains.
	20873	Private	Richardson, T.	Wounded. Moislains.
	345457	Private	Robertson, A.G.	Wounded. Moislains.
	22178	Private	Rutherford, J.	Wounded. Moislains.
	21831	Private	Rutherford, P.	Wounded. Moislains.
	240382	Private	Scott, A.	Wounded. Moislains.
	2901	Private	Scott, W.	Wounded. Moislains.
	345685	Private	Simpson, T.	Wounded. Moislains.
	345807	Private	Smart, J.	Wounded. Died of wounds 4.10.18.
	345412	Private	Smeaton, W.	Wounded. Moislains.
	18102	Private	Smith, J.	Wounded. Died of wounds 2.9.18.
	346043	Private	Smith, W.	Wounded. Moislains.
	345209	Private	Spence, T.	Wounded. Moislains.
	22230	Private	Stewart, G.C.	Wounded. Moislains.
	21843	Private	Stewart, H.	Wounded. Moislains.
	345931	Private	Stewart, J.	Wounded. Moislains.
	22159	Private	Sturrock, D.K.	Wounded. Moislains.
	22155	Private	Summers, G.	Wounded. Moislains.

Date	Number	Rank	Name	Status
2.9.18	17654	Private	Tallent, J.	Wounded. Moislains.
	345147	Private	Thomson, G.	Wounded. Moislains.
	203426	Private	Tod, D.	Wounded. Moislains.
	267695	Private	Turnbull, J.	Wounded. Moislains.
	21832	Private	Twaddle, J.	Wounded. Moislains.
	19848	Private	Twist, J.	Wounded. Moislains.
	345743	Private	Walkenshaw, A.	Wounded. Moislains.
	17817	Private	Walker, J.	Wounded. Moislains.
	20325	Private	Watson, R.	Wounded. Moislains.
	345745	Private	Wheeler, J.	Wounded. Moislains.
	345389	Private	Whitehead, J.	Wounded. Moislains.
	340024	Private	Whyte, J.	Wounded. Moislains.
	20392	Private	Williams, E.	Wounded. Moislains.
	346022	Private	Williams, H.	Wounded. Moislains.
	20363	Private	Wilson, J.	Wounded. Moislains.
	345146	Private	Wilson, R.	Wounded. Moislains.
	6949	Private	Wilson, W.	Wounded. Moislains.
	15883	Private	Yacamini, R.	Wounded. Moislains.

Date	Number	Name	Rank	Remarks
2.9.18	22331	Gunn, G.	Private	Wounded and missing.
		M'Lean, J.	2nd Lieut.	Wounded and at duty.
		Brodie Brown, T.	2nd Lieut.	Wounded and at duty.
		Cruickshank, I.W.	2nd Lieut.	Wounded and at duty.
	345943	Campbell, D.	Sergt.	Wounded and at duty.
	345660	Boylan, J.	Private	Wounded and at duty.
	345870	Horne, W.	Private	Wounded and at duty.
	20389	Kearsey, A.G.	Private	Wounded and at duty.
	21855	Livingstone, A.	Private	Wounded and at duty.
3.9.18		Drysdale, J.C.	Lieut.	Wounded.
9.9.18	21839	Robb, J.	Private	Wounded and at duty. St Emilie.
10.9.18	345125	Ritchie, J.W.	Cpl.	Killed. St Emilie.
	15546	Davidson, J.	Private	Killed. St Emilie.
	345959	Dawson, J.	Private	Killed. St Emilie.
	22147	Donaldson, T.	Private	Killed. St Emilie.
	340017	Ford, J.	Private	Killed. St Emilie.
	345253	Geekie, J.A.P.	Private	Killed. St Emilie.
	20365	Halliday, D.	Private	Killed. St Emilie.

Date	Number	Rank	Name	Status
10.9.18	345659	Private	Martin, W.	Killed. St Emilie.
	203406	Private	Munro, W.	Killed. St Emilie.
	43045	Private	Nairn, J.	Killed. St Emilie.
	340007	Private	O'Key, J.	Killed. St Emilie.
	345978	Private	Rennie, H.	Killed. St Emilie.
	346033	Private	Slater, J.	Killed. St Emilie.
	20361	Private	Smith, R.	Killed. St Emilie.
	15545	Private	Younger, C.	Killed. St Emilie.
	345092	L/Cpl.	Coupar, D.L.	Missing, presumed killed. St Emilie.
	41665	Private	M'Connachie, W.	Missing, presumed killed. St Emilie.
	21830	Private	Perston, W.	Missing, presumed killed. St Emilie.
	345313	Private	Ramsay, J.W.	Missing, presumed killed. St Emilie.
		2nd Lieut.	M'Lean, J.	Wounded. St Emilie.
		2nd Lieut.	Cruickshank, I.W.	Wounded. St Emilie.
	345946	Sergt.	Mackie, A.	Wounded. St Emilie.
	345054	Cpl.	Fleming, A.	Wounded. St Emilie.
	345684	Cpl.	Smart, A.	Wounded. St Emilie.
	345376	L/Cpl.	Cooper, A.	Wounded. St Emilie.

194

Date	Number	Rank	Name	Remarks
10.9.18	345869	L/Cpl.	Craig, J.	Wounded. St Emilie.
	345391	Private	Bett, J.	Wounded. St Emilie.
	345258	Private	Boath, L.	Wounded. St Emilie.
	310082	Private	Brebner, C.	Died of wounds 10.9.18. St Emilie.
	345957	Private	Cameron, W.	Wounded. St Emilie.
	18316	Private	Dorward, W.	Wounded. St Emilie.
	345309	Private	Henderson, J.	Wounded. St Emilie.
	345610	Private	Laing, T.	Wounded. St Emilie.
	18799	Private	Lowson, D.	Died of wounds 11.9.18. St Emilie.
	345034	Private	Peter, D.S.	Wounded. St Emilie.
	345556	Private	Robertson, J.	Wounded. St Emilie.
	20367	Private	Robin, D.	Wounded. St Emilie.
	20390	Private	Roper, J.	Died of wounds 11.9.18. St Emilie.
	17741	Private	Sharp, W.	Wounded. St Emilie.
	350163	Private	Thomson, C.	Wounded. St Emilie.
	21676	Private	Wallace, J.	Wounded. St Emilie.
	345114	Private	Wilson, A.	Wounded. St Emilie.
	345672	Private	Wylie, H.	Wounded. St Emilie.

Date	Number	Rank	Name	Remarks
10.9.18	22190	Private	Young, W.	Wounded. St Emilie.
	345947	Sergt.	M'Gregor, H.	Prisoner of war.
	345106	Sergt.	M'Lellan, J.R.	Prisoner of war.
	345637	Cpl.	Davidson, D.	Prisoner of war.
	345231	Private	Annand, A.A.	Prisoner of war.
	345934	Private	Davidson, R.	Prisoner of war.
	20136	Private	Gray, D.	Prisoner of war.
	345103	Private	Greig, J.R.	Prisoner of war.
	340005	Private	Henderson, J.F.	Prisoner of war.
	345927	Private	M'Killop, D.	Prisoner of war. Wounded.
	16473	Private	Nisbet, R.	Prisoner of war. Wounded.
	30372	Private	Sharp, M.	Prisoner of war. Wounded.
	22206	Private	Wilson, W.A.	Prisoner of war. Wounded.
	345153	Private	Henderson, J.	Wounded and at duty. St Emilie.
18.9.18	200328	Private	Bonnar, G.	Killed.
	345266	Private	M'Donald, A.	Killed.
	18460	Private	M'Lean, J.	Killed.
		2nd Lieut.	Stuart, H.C.	Wounded.

Date	Number	Rank	Name	Status
18.9.18	345400	L/Cpl.	Henderson, A.	Wounded.
	345428	Private	Beal, J.	Wounded.
	345917	Private	Cairncross, H.	Wounded.
	345312	Private	Calderhead, J.	Wounded.
	24486	Private	Campbell, D.	Wounded.
	345591	Private	Cummings, J.	Wounded.
	22915	Private	Gordon, C.	Wounded.
	23586	Private	Greenwood, J.	Wounded.
	41264	Private	Ireland, P.	Wounded.
	2439	Private	Kelly, T.	Wounded.
	40294	Private	M'Donald, A.	Wounded.
	345791	Private	M'Hardy, A.	Wounded.
	20486	Private	M'Kenzie, R.	Wounded.
	345184	Private	Maloney, J.	Died of wounds 29.9.18.
	41060	Private	Mann, R.	Wounded.
	345971	Private	Marshall, J.	Wounded.
	345690	Private	Meldrum, F.	Wounded.
	345046	Private	Nicoll, R.	Wounded.

Date	Number	Rank	Name	Status
18.9.18	345163	Private	Ramage, J.	Wounded.
	345474	Private	Smart, A.	Wounded.
	345501	Private	Soutar, W.	Wounded.
	345068	Private	Storrar, M.	Wounded.
	6630	Private	Strachan, D.	Wounded.
	14374	Private	Walker, J.	Wounded.
20.9.18	22158	Private	Grant, R.	Wounded.
21.9.18	18725	Private	Cant, A.	Killed.
	22151	Private	Cubbon, E.	Killed.
	340025	Private	Easson, W.	Killed.
	346049	Private	Forbes, J.A.	Killed.
	25324	Private	Morrison, D.L.	Killed.
	346034	Cpl.	Thom, J.	Wounded.
	14766	Private	Bain, A.	Wounded.
	345967	Private	M'Crae, M.	Wounded.
	22191	Private	Penman, J.	Wounded.
	25317	Private	Philp, A.	Wounded.
	345364	Private	Summers, R.	Wounded.

Date	Number	Rank	Name	Remarks
21.9.18	345102	Private	M'Dougal, G.	Wounded and at duty.
22.9.18	345220	Private	Lessells, W.	Killed.
		2nd Lieut.	Innes, D. M'L.	Wounded. Died of wounds 7.10.18.
	7206	C.Q.M.S.	Elder, J.	Wounded.
	18322	Cpl.	Smith, R.	Wounded.
	15110	L/Cpl.	Livingstone, E.	Wounded.
	202414	L/Cpl.	Rader, J.	Wounded.
	2929	Private	Birrell, D.	Wounded.
	18699	Private	Condie, M.	Wounded.
	213313	Private	Cooper, J.	Wounded.
	345818	Private	Etchels, T.	Wounded.
	345607	Private	Finnigan, R.	Wounded.
	20754	Private	Grierson, W.	Wounded.
	240503	Private	Hunter, A.S.	Wounded.
	25317	Private	Philip, A.	Wounded.
	7536	Private	Pringle, J.	Wounded.
	25326	Private	Rankine, W.	Wounded.
	25448	Private	Reid, E.	Wounded.

Date	Number	Rank	Name	Status
22.9.18	25316	Private	Ritchie, J.	Wounded.
	25365	Private	Robertson, J.	Wounded.
	25348	Private	Strachan, T.	Wounded.
	345783	Private	M'Aree, A.	Wounded and at duty.
23.9.18	25217	Private	Smart, J.	Killed.
	25451	Private	Allan, R.	Wounded.
	25452	Private	Gilchrist, J.	Wounded.
	25344	Private	Inglis, R.V.	Wounded.
24.9.18	S/22207	Private	Coutts, A.G.	Killed.
	S/22027	Private	Inglis, J.	Killed.
		2nd Lieut.	Fell, F.J.	Wounded.
	24050	Private	Appleby, H.	Wounded.
	293071	Private	Boath, W.	Wounded.
	16545	Private	Craik, A.	Wounded.
	22148	Private	Henderson, D.	Wounded.
	203189	Private	M'Donald, J.R.	Wounded. Died of wounds 25.9.18.
	17064	Private	Minchella, P.	Wounded.
	25402	Private	Wallace, D.	Wounded.

Date	Number	Rank	Name	Remarks
15.10.18		2nd Lieut.	Stevenson, E.J.	Wounded.
	345958	Private	Christison, G.	Wounded.
	345925	Private	Guthrie, J.	Wounded.
	6007	Private	Laird, W.	Wounded.
16.10.18	345662	Private	M'Kendrick, A.	Killed.
	345979	Private	Ross, T.	Killed.
		Lieut.	Ewart, R.H.	Wounded. Died of wounds 16.10.18.
		2nd Lieut.	Wood, A.R., D.C.M., M.M.	Wounded. Died of wounds 16.10.18.
	345018	C.S.M.	Henderson, W.	Wounded. Died of wounds 16.10.18.
	293071	L/Cpl.	Boath, W.	Wounded. Died of wounds 16.10.18.
	345403	Private	Gilmour, A.	Wounded. Died of wounds 16.10.18.
	345323	Private	Goodall, J.	Wounded. Died of wounds 16.10.18.
	13428	Private	Ross, A.	Wounded. Died of wounds 16.10.18.
	21686	Private	Sharp, A.	Wounded. Died of wounds 16.10.18.
	25377	Private	Barclay, L.	Wounded and at duty.
	345456	Private	Mitchell, D.	Wounded and at duty.
	5116	Private	Skinner, E.	Wounded and at duty.
21.10.18	19537	Private	Haggart, J.	Killed.

Date	No.	Rank	Name	Remarks
21.10.18	7817	L/Cpl.	Anderson, W.	Wounded.
	202903	Private	Adams, C.	Wounded.
	17894	Private	Bruce, D.	Wounded.
	21184	Private	Laird, J.	Wounded.
	21152	Private	Lally, D.	Wounded.
	268963	Private	M'Gee, A.B.	Wounded.
	21100	Private	Penny, E.	Wounded.
	315708	Private	Simpson, T.	Wounded.
22.10.18	345055	Sergt.	Bayne, A.	Wounded. Died of wounds 22.10.18.
	345321	Private	Ramsay, J.	Wounded. Died of wounds 22.10.18.
23.10.18		2nd Lieut.	Cumming, F.K.	Killed.
	26870	L/Cpl.	Izatt, R., M.M.	Killed.
	25462	Private	Barber, J.	Killed.
	9729	Private	Bartie, T.	Killed.
	15814	Private	Campbell, J.	Killed.
	12506	Private	Cockburn, T.	Killed.
	6158	Private	Sowerby, E.	Killed.
	25347	Private	Walker, T.	Killed.

Date	No.	Rank	Name	Remarks
23.10.18	25378	Private	Webb, A.	Killed.
		2nd Lieut.	Robertson, R.	Wounded.
	345943	Sergt.	Campbell, D.	Wounded.
	345490	L/Cpl.	Crawford, D.	Wounded.
	25376	L/Cpl.	Patterson, R.	Wounded.
	6006	L/Cpl.	Spence, W.	Wounded.
	14539	Private	Anderson, D.	Wounded. Died of wounds 26.10.18.
	6145	Private	Black, P.	Wounded. Died of wounds 26.10.18.
	25199	Private	Conway, J.	Wounded. Died of wounds 26.10.18.
	25719	Private	Davidson, R.	Wounded. Died of wounds 26.10.18.
	345818	Private	Etchels, T.	Wounded.
	5950	Private	Kemp, A.	Wounded.
	5255	Private	M'Dougall, A.	Wounded.
	6176	Private	M'Ilroy, B.	Wounded.
	25346	Private	M'Kay, H.	Wounded.
	203311	Private	M'Lean, D.	Wounded.
	16171	Private	Reekie, J.	Wounded.
	25656	Private	Rough, D.	Wounded.

Date	Number	Rank	Name	Remarks
23.10.18	14611	Private	Russell, A.	Wounded.
	267921	Private	Scott, W.	Wounded.
	25368	Private	Stevenson, G.	Wounded.
	43388	Private	Swift, J.	Wounded. Died of wounds 24.10.18.
		2nd Lieut.	Mathewson, J.S.	Wounded and at duty.
	345074	Sergt.	Leitch, J.J.	Wounded and at duty.
	20377	L/Cpl.	Sinclair, J.	Wounded and at duty.
	340030	Private	M'Donell, D.	Wounded and at duty.
	345982	Private	Robertson, A.	Wounded and at duty.
	290566	Private	Watson, R.B.	Wounded and at duty.
1.11.18		Captain	Colthart, R.H.	Wounded. Died of wounds 2.11.18.
	345298	Cpl.	Matthew, R.	Wounded.
	14770	Private	Craig, D.	Wounded.
	345770	Private	Nicol, A.	Wounded.
	345211	Private	O'Malley, J.	Wounded and at duty.
14.4.18	345305	Private	Morrison, G.	Died of disease.
4.1.18	345881	Private	Melville, C.	Died of disease.
1.2.18	265831	Private	Walker, H.	Died of disease.

TOTAL CASUALTIES.

OFFICERS.

Killed	12
Died of wounds	9
Wounded	32
Wounded and remaining at duty	5
	58

N.C.Os. AND MEN.

Killed	188
Died of wounds	46
Missing	5
Died of disease	15
Drowned	16
Wounded	568
Wounded and remaining at duty	52
Prisoners of war	20
	910

Grand Total	**968**